GET A GRIP ON YOUR MONEY

A Teen Study in
Christian Financial Management

Larry Burkett

Focus on the Family Publishing
Pomona, California 91799

First printing, 1990
Printed in the United States of America
Edited by Dave and Neta Jackson

Larry Burkett
GET A GRIP ON YOUR MONEY: A Teen Study in Christian Financial Management

Summary: A course on managing personal finances designed for teens' individual or classroom use. Emphasis is on using Christian principles in budgeting, writing a resume, and applying for a job.

Focus on the Family Publishing
Rolf Zettersten, Vice President
Wes Haystead, Curriculum Editor
Dean Merrill, Vice President, Communications
Dave and Neta Jackson, Contributing Editors
Illustrations, David Slonim
Design, Jerry Price
ISBN 0-929608-75-5

CONTENTS

Introduction

Lessons:

1. Choosing a Career   **1**

2. Balancing Your Budget   **7**

3. Setting Up Your Records   **13**

4. Balancing a Checking Account   **23**

5. Loans and Credit Cards   **27**

6. Coping with Budget Busters   **37**

7. Understanding Insurance   **43**

8. Buying Cars   **47**

9. Buying a First Home   **55**

10. Looking for Work   **63**

11. Writing a Sharp Resume   **71**

12. The Winning Job Interview   **77**

13. Giving to God   **83**

Appendix:
A Job Descriptions   **91**
B Budget Needs   **93**
C Budget Busters   **103**
D Loan Table   **105**
E Monthly Expenses   **107**

Forms 1-11 (Reproducible Pages)   **115**

Quiz Answers   **127**

INTRODUCTION

Have you ever dreamed of having All the Money You Need? Most people could realize that dream if they knew how. And it can come true for you, too!

In this country, except when there are major economic upheavals or the collapse of large industries, there are only three things you must do to have all the money you need:

1. Get a good job,
2. Be a diligent worker, and
3. Manage your money wisely.

This course will help you learn how to do all three, but the emphasis is on money management—the place where most people fail.

To begin, notice that I said All the Money You NEED, not All the Money You WANT. That's an important distinction, and at first it may disappoint you if you were dreaming about a big yacht or three months of skiing in the Alps every year. But wait.

Isn't having all the money you need a whole lot better than struggling month after month to avoid bankruptcy and to keep bill collectors from turning off your heat or repossessing your car? Isn't it better than ending up in divorce court because you and your spouse were never able to work out your money problems?

This course uses a simulation method for learning how to manage money. Many universities use this method to train students in their future vocations. The purpose is to reproduce, as closely as possible, the actual conditions you will face later. This involves paying taxes, buying homes, cars, clothes, etc. In this study you will learn how to plan and prepare a budget as well as select the right home to fit your budget. Also, you'll learn how to choose the right life insurance and what it means to pay simple or add-on interest when you buy a car.

You may be thinking, 'What do I need this for?' But you do. Financial problems contribute to nearly 90 percent of all the divorces in America. Virtually none of those people thought financial problems would destroy their marriages. The vast majority made their mistakes simply out of ignorance.

Prerequisites:

This study contains all the information necessary to develop and maintain a working budget. You should use an inexpensive pocket calculator to do all your math computations for keeping a budget. While the arithmetic is simple, sharpening those skills is not the primary object of this course. On the other hand, error-free calculations are essential.

Also, you may need to obtain the use of a photocopying machine to make copies of the forms in the back of this book. Do not work directly on these masters, so that you can always make more copies if you mess up a form. (If you are using this book as part of a class group, your teacher may provide the copies you need.)

The first column of "number of copies" is if you intend to keep a budget for one month only. The second column shows the number of copies needed to complete the "For Additional Study" section in each lesson and thereby keep a simulated budget for the equivalent of six months. The "one month only" plan will acquaint you with all the major ideas in this course. The "six month" plan will firmly ingrain these ideas into your money-handling patterns enabling you to truly "get a grip on your money."

Form Number	Title	Number of Copies	
		1 mo.	6 mo.
Form 1	Monthly Income and Expenses	4	4
Form 2	Division of Pay	2	2
Form 3	Individual Account Sheet	12	72
Form 4	Bank Deposits	1	3
Form 5	Blank Checks	10	60
Form 6	Checking Account Reconciliation	1	6
Form 7	Loan Applications	1	1
Form 8	Insurance Needs Worksheet	1	1
Form 9	Creating Your Resumé	1	1

Group Study:

A teacher's guide is available for this study. It is necessary to direct classroom participation, and it contains materials needed for group activities. It provides a variety of jobs and budget selections as well as masters for all the forms needed by students.

Independent Study:

If you are doing this study alone, follow the instructions given in each lesson. The appendixes and forms provide everything you need to complete the course.

CHOOSING A CAREER

GETTING STARTED

Having all the money you need often has more to do with how you manage your money than how much you earn. This is why many people continue to have money problems even though their income increases year after year. For them, there never seems to be enough. Even if their salary doubled, they would soon think they needed "just a little more."

You can learn how to avoid that trap. This session will introduce you to one of the most helpful tools in managing your money: careful budgeting. In order to manage your money, you must be able to plan where you want it to go.

For this course you will select a "job" along with its salary. It will provide all the money you need for this course, provided you manage it carefully. NOTE: The dollar figures used in the examples are based on national averages and may vary significantly from actual income and expense levels in your area. While it will be helpful for you to investigate the actual costs of living in your area, keep your focus on learning the process rather than on the specific dollar amounts.

Enjoy the process!

In this lesson you will . . .
- Select a career and its associated salary, taxes, etc.;
- Determine what your net spendable income will be after taxes and charitable giving;
- Estimate what percentage of your budget you want to spend for such basic categories as a home, car, clothes, vacation, etc.

STEP 1
Choosing Your Job

If you are a part of a class group, your leader has a variety of jobs from which to choose. Your salary will be revealed after you select the job. Keep in mind, with higher pay there often come increased taxes, professional expenses, and other responsibilities.

If you are doing an individual study, you will find two jobs

listed in Appendix A at the back of this book. Choose one of them.

Take note of:
- your salary,
- tax rate,
- the cash assets you have in savings (available for down payments on a house and a car),
- the sample paycheck showing the actual amount you will need to budget twice a month.

On a copy of Form 1, "Monthly Income and Expenses," enter your job number, your title, your annual income, and monthly income—your annual salary divided by twelve. (Masters for photocopying the forms are in the back of this book. Do not write on the masters. Only fill out the copies!)

Example:

Monthly Income and Expenses		FORM 1
Job Name *Pilot* # *1*	**7. Debts (5%)**	_____
Annual Income *$30,000*	Credit Cards	_____
Monthly Income *$ 2,500*	Loans & Notes	_____
	Other	

STEP 2
Determining Net Spendable Income

Budgeting each month will be based on your net spendable income (NSI). This is your monthly salary, less your charitable contributions and taxes.

Most charitable contributions can be tax deductible at the time you calculate your income tax. They must be given to a nonprofit, charitable, religious, or educational group that meets government guidelines. "Tax deductible" means that the amount is subtracted from your gross (or total) income before you calculate your annual tax bill.

The government permits these deductions because society encourages charitable giving which benefits the public good. It can be a more personal way of caring for needy people and for advancing worthwhile ventures than government programs. Plus, it fosters a kind and generous populace. You may enter any amount—or nothing—in the "charitable contributions" category, based upon your own convictions.

However taxes are not an option. The tax category includes federal, state and FICA (Social Security). Your estimated tax liability is shown with the information for your job.

Subtract any charitable contributions and taxes from your monthly income. The answer is your Net Spendable Income (NSI).

Example:

```
                                              FORM 1
        Monthly Income and Expenses

Job Name  Pilot          # 1        7. Debts (5%)          _____
Annual Income        $30,000           Credit Cards   _____
Monthly Income       $ 2,500           Loans & Notes  _____
                                       Other          _____
LESS
  1. Charitable Contributions $ 250   8. Enter. & Recreation (7%)  $ 105
  2. Tax                      $ 750      Eating Out     $ 32
                                         Trips          _____
NET SPENDABLE INCOME       $ 1,500       Babysitters    _____
                                         Activities# R-4    25
  3. Housing # H-1  (30%)  $ 420         Vacation# V-6      48
```

STEP 3
Estimating Budget Percentages

You will notice on Form 1 that categories 3—12 have a percentage shown in parentheses next to each category. These are guidelines, adding up to 100 percent of the NSI. The amount you choose to spend in each category may vary, but your total should also add up to 100 percent, or your budget will not balance.

Below are the suggested ranges for each category. They are in relation to your NSI, not total income.

SAMPLE BUDGET PERCENTAGES

Category	Percentages
3. Housing (Total)	30%—36%
4. Food	12%—17%
5. Auto (Total)	15%—20%
6. Insurance	3%—7%
7. Debts	5%—6%
8. Entertainment	5%—8%
9. Clothing	5%—6%
10. Savings	5%
11. Medical Expenses	4%—8%
12. Miscellaneous	5%—10%

On scratch paper list the percentage you would like to set for each category in your budget. Begin by giving those categories most important to you the higher percentages—and the least important ones lower percentages. For instance, if a nice car is more important to you than entertainment, then go for the higher percentage for auto and the lower percentage for entertainment.

Adjust these percentages by increasing some and lowering others until they total 100 percent.

Next, write the dollar equivalent of your NSI for each percentage: multiply your NSI by each category's percentage.

For example: If your NSI is $1,500 per month and you selected the sample percentages used on Form 1, your calculations would be:

SAMPLE BUDGET PERCENTAGES AND DOLLAR AMOUNTS

Category	NSI		Percentage		Amount
3. Housing (Total)	$1,500	x	30%	=	$450
4. Food	1,500	x	16%	=	240
5. Auto (Total)	1,500	x	15%	=	225
6. Insurance	1,500	x	5%	=	75
7. Debts	1,500	x	5%	=	75
8. Entertainment	1,500	x	7%	=	105
9. Clothing	1,500	x	5%	=	75
10. Savings	1,500	x	5%	=	75
11. Medical Expenses	1,500	x	5%	=	75
12. Miscellaneous	1,500	x	7%	=	105
TOTALS			100%		$1,500

At this point you have not accumulated any debt, so you do not have to allow the 5-6 percent for that amount. Adding that amount to your savings would build a cushion to help you avoid going into debt in the future.

Or, with no debts, the 5 percent assigned to category 7 ($1,500 x 5% = $75.00) could be moved to another category. For example, you could then spend $525 per month on housing. Just keep in mind that it is wise to avoid debt. (The topic of borrowing will be studied in Lesson 5.)

Continue adjusting your percentages until they total 100 percent and your total amount of cash shown in all the categories is equal to your NSI. Be sure to save your concluding amounts for the next lesson as they will be your guidelines for making economic life-style choices.

This Is Your Life

Applying what you learn to your present finances.

(Although these lessons simulate financial decisions you will face in the future, doing the following will help you apply what you're learning to your present money management. Keep all work done in this section in a separate folder.)

Do you know how much money you make in a year? How much you spend on clothes. . .pizza. . .gas and bus fare? Are you always out of money and having to borrow from friends?

In order to have the necessary facts to "have all the money you need" right now and help you set up a personal budget, do the following:

1. Estimate your personal monthly income from all sources—from job, parents, gifts, etc. Multiply by twelve to see what your estimated yearly income is. For example, an average of $35 per month equals $425 for the year ($35x12).

2. Determine the money you have to spend each month (your Net Spendable Income): subtract any charitable gifts and any taxes that are withheld. (Look for federal, state, and FICA withholdings on a paycheck stub.)

3. Identify the budget categories for your current and desired expenditures (i.e., clothing, food, entertainment, transportation, savings, etc.). Estimate the percentages and amounts you want to spend in each category, making sure the totals do not exceed 100%.

4. If accurately estimating your income and expenses is hard, you need to keep track of all actual income you receive for one month, and all actual expenditures. Do this simply by keeping a notebook handy and recording income on one page and a running list of all money spent and for what on another page. (Sound like busy-work? Knowing where the money goes is vital when learning to manage your money.)

FOR ADDITIONAL STUDY

1. Interview one full-time wage earner who keeps an accurate budget and is willing to share about his or her spending patterns. Record how much (and what percentage of NSI) he or she spends in categories 3—12 mentioned above (as closely as they compare). Also, note whether the person has any other significant categories and the amounts (and percentages) in them.

2. Study Appendix B, "Budget Needs," which includes the choices available to you for each budget category. This will help you make better-informed choices in the next lesson.

3. Identify three jobs that would interest you as a long-term career. Then from the help-wanted ads in a local newspaper, determine the current salary range for those jobs in your part of the country. List any factors (experience, academic degrees, licenses, etc.) which influence salary level.

BALANCING YOUR BUDGET

GETTING STARTED

Most of us would rather have a four-bedroom home with a pool than a two-bedroom apartment with no air-conditioning. We would rather drive around in a Turbo Porsche than a Ford Escort. Still, each decision must be tempered by realistic planning. If you can learn the rules now while the losses are on paper, you will avoid years of grief later when the losses could wreck your life.

STEP 1
Making Choices Within Your Budget Categories

In the last lesson you estimated how much you could spend in each budget category while still keeping your budget in balance. To do this, you first arrived at a percentage for each category. Then you multiplied that percentage by your NSI (Net Spendable Income) to find the dollar amount available for that category.

In this lesson you will . . .
- **Determine your economic life-style by making choices within your budget categories;**
- **Make sure that your budget balances;**
- **Learn how to budget your monthly expenses to coincide with multiple pay periods in the month.**

Now that you know approximately how much you can spend in each category, it's time to "go shopping" for the options you want. Appendix B in the back of this book offers a variety of options for most categories. Appendix E is a helpful guide.

    A. Select one item from each listed category.
    B. Write in the number/name on a copy of Form 1.
    C. Then fill in the amount as designated.

For housing and auto selections you can only choose purchases for which you have sufficient down payments. The "cash" you have saved was designated with your Job Description, Appendix A.

For those categories where no options are given (food, savings, medical) use the percentage/dollar amounts you have calculated from your NSI. (Example: Food=17% of $1500 NSI: $255.)

Be sure to select only one item per category.

Example:

FORM 1

Monthly Income and Expenses

Job Name *Pilot*   # *1*
Annual Income   *$30,000*
Monthly Income   *$ 2,500*

LESS
1. Charitable Contributions   *$ 250*
2. Tax   *$ 750*

NET SPENDABLE INCOME   *$ 1,500*

3. Housing # *H-1* (30%)   *$ 420*
   Mortgage (rent) *$ 275*
   Insurance *25*
   Taxes
   Electricity *70*
   Gas
   Water
   Sanitation
   Telephone *50*
   Maintenance
   Other

4. Food (17%)   *$ 255*

5. Auto(s) # *A-8* (15%)   *$ 225*
   Payments *$ 65*
   Gas & Oil *50*
   Insurance *25*
   License *10*
   Taxes
   Maint./Repair/
     Replacement *75*

6. Insurance (5%)   *$ 80*
   Life# *LI-6* *$ 20*
   Medical# *MI-5* *60*

   Other#

7. **Debts (5%)**
   Credit Cards
   Loans & Notes
   Other

8. **Enter. & Recreation (7%)**   *$ 105*
   Eating Out *$ 32*
   Trips
   Babysitters
   Activities# *R-4* *25*
   Vacation# *V-6* *48*

   Other

9. **Clothing #_____ (5%)**   *$ 75*

10. **Savings (5%)**   *$ 75*

11. **Medical Expenses (5%)**   *$ 75*
    Doctor *$ 25*
    Dental *25*
    Drugs *15*
    Other *10*

12. **Miscellaneous (6%)**   *$ 140*
    Toiletry, cosmetics *$ 10*
    Beauty, barber *20*
    Laundry, cleaning *20*
    Allowances,
      lunches *35*
    Subscriptions *5*
    Gifts
      (incl. Christmas) *20*
    Special Education
    Cash *30*
    Other

TOTAL EXPENSES   *$ 1450*

Net Spendable Income   *$ 1500*

Difference   *+$50*

STEP 2
Adjustments

You may discover that some items you want cost more than the amount you have budgeted for that category. Where that is the case, you will need to make some decisions. You must lower your expectations or adjust the amount you intended to spend in other categories so you can add more funds to this category. **Make any adjustments needed to make your budget amounts realistic.**

When you think everything fits within your budget, **do a final sum of all the category expenses to be sure that the total**

remains within your NSI. The bottom line is: your budget must balance.

LAST CHANCE: If your budget does not balance, this is your last chance to trade for less costly items.

STEP 3
Locking in Your Budget

In making your selections and adjustments for each category, your Form 1, "Monthly Income and Expenses," has probably become rather messy. Therefore, **take the time to redo Form 1 by copying the contents onto a fresh copy of Form 1.**

One reminder: except for Category 7 (Debt), you must budget something for each category 2—12. You will be required to handle expenses in each category through the course of this study. Failure to budget will create a debt.

STEP 4
Division of Pay

In reality, people get paid a myriad of ways—weekly, every two weeks, monthly, etc. The sample paycheck in Appendix A illustrates a twice-monthly pay period. In this study, you will need to manage a twice-monthly paycheck.

Therefore, you will need to divide your expenses so that the payments are balanced. You will pay half your bills and make half your purchases in the beginning of the month and the other half near the end. Of course some expenses, like food, are consistent throughout the month, so you must spend some for food in each half.

Using Form 2, "Division of Pay," divide your allocation of pay so that your payments and income balance.

NOTE: Your total housing allowance must be taken out of the first paycheck. This is because the payments are due before the fifteenth of the month, which is the next pay period. To accomplish this large payment, the example on the next page shifts most of the car allocation, insurance, entertainment, clothing, etc., to the second pay period.

Keep this payment schedule in mind when negotiating a car loan. You might need to arrange the payment date for the sixteenth or later. See the example on the next page.

Example:

DIVISION OF PAY   FORM 2

PER YEAR $ _30,000_

PER MONTH $ _2,500_   DIVISION OF PAY
                            PER PAY PERIOD $ _1,250_

MONTHLY PAYMENT CATEGORY	$ 1,250 1st PAY PERIOD	$ 1,250 2nd PAY PERIOD
1. Charitable Contributions	# 125	# 125
2. Taxes	375	375
NET SPENDABLE INCOME (PER MONTH)	$ 750	$ 750
3. Housing	420	-0-
4. Food	120	120
5. Automobile(s)	50	175
6. Insurance	-0-	80
7. Debts	-0-	-0-
8. Enter. & Recreation	32	73
9. Clothing	-0-	75
10. Savings	-0-	75
11. Medical	25	50
12. Miscellaneous	75	80
TOTALS (Items 3 through 12)	$ 722	$ 728

STEP 5
Calculating Irregular Expenses

Irregular or non-monthly expenses are handled in a different way. In your budget the irregular expenses such as vacations, dentist, doctor, etc., have been allocated monthly by percentage. In real life, it doesn't always work out that neatly. Someone may be over-spending without knowing it, because they have no vacation budget. Then, when they take one, there's no money reserved for that purpose, so they charge much of the cost on their credit cards. When the bills come in, they are difficult to pay.

The way to avoid this problem is to estimate how much you expect to spend in an area, then divide that by twelve to arrive at your monthly average. Better yet, once you have kept records for the past year, use those as a more realistic source for estimating the annual cost. Then put that amount in savings each month to prepare for when the expense must be paid.

Example:

	Estimated Cost			Per Month
1. Vacation	$600	÷ 12	=	$50
2. Dentist	$300	÷ 12	=	$25
3. Doctor	$300	÷ 12	=	$25
4. Automobile	$2,640	÷ 12	=	$220
5. Annual Insurance				
(Life)	$180	÷ 12	=	$15
(Health)	$600	÷ 12	=	$50
(Auto)	$300	÷ 12	=	$25
(Home)	$300	÷ 12	=	$25
6. Clothing	$1,020	÷ 12	=	$85

This Is Your Life

Applying what you learn to your present finances.

1. You've done one week of recording actual income and expenditures? Continue keeping track in your personal notebook. Remember the goal is to list all actual income and spending for a full month.

2. Using a copy of Form 1 ("Monthly Income and Expenses") as a guide, list your estimated monthly income, charitable contributions, taxes, and Net Spendable Income at the top. (The results from "This Is Your Life," Lesson 1.) Then make a list of the real expense categories you normally face in a month—e.g., Food, Fun, Transportation, School, Clothes, Savings, Miscellaneous, etc. (Don't try to figure percentages or fill in amounts—that will come later.)

3. If you have a job, how often do you receive a paycheck? Fill out an extra copy of Form 2, "Division of Pay." What does each paycheck usually get spent for? (Do you spend paycheck #1 and save #2? Are you always out of money and having to borrow from parents and friends—then spend your paychecks paying people back? Be honest!)

4. Think ahead. What irregular expenses pop up during a year: summer activities? special clothes or equipment for sports? school clothes in September? How do you usually meet those needs financially? (Do your parents kick in? Do you get an extra job, go in debt, use your savings?)

FOR ADDITIONAL STUDY

1. Ask your parents or someone else if you can review their bills for electricity or heat for the last year. Usually, these will vary from month to month because of the fluctuations in the weather. Record the bills for each month, then establish the average monthly cost. (Some utility companies allow their established customers to pay equal monthly payments throughout the year so that costs don't fluctuate drastically.)

2. Suppose you have charged a $1,130 vacation on your MasterCard and a new bedroom set for $1,300 at Sears. Your combined monthly payments on these debts equals $90. (Charge card interest rates are usually very high. The monthly payment above is calculated at 19.8 percent annual interest over a three-year repayment period.) On a fresh copy of Form 1, "Monthly Income and Expenses," recalculate your categories.

   a. First fill in $90 under Category 7.
   b. Figure its percentage of your NSI. (If your NSI was $1,500, the equation would be $90 ÷ $1,500 = 6%).
   c. Reduce other category percentages to allow for this percentage. (For instance, if your debt equals 6 percent, you will need to reduce one or more categories by a total of that many percentage points.)
   d. Recalculate the dollar value for each category you have changed.
   e. Check to see that your percentages total 100 percent and that the dollar value of all categories does not exceed your NSI.
   f. Decide what spending changes you will make to remain within that amount. Will you have to live in a less costly house, cut back on entertainment and recreation, or what?

Notice how the implications of debt affect your freedom in other areas. Also, you might be interested in knowing that besides repaying your debt, you would have to pay an additional $810 in interest on these purchases before you were debt-free. Can you think of better things to do with that money?

SETTING UP YOUR RECORDS

GETTING STARTED

Suppose you are trying to decide whether you can afford a new TV. The local discount appliance store is having a "midnight madness sale," and the new Motorola that you want is on sale for $239.95. Things have been going fairly well. You've paid the mortgage this month and are up to date on all your other bills and still have $289.32.

Should you do it?

At first it looks good. Then you remember that you saved some of your funds for other purposes. For two months you haven't had any medical expenses—that accounts for $150. Your miscellaneous expenses haven't been as high as you anticipated, so you've saved there. Still, there's that vacation for which you've been saving. Part of the money should go for it. But how much?

One of the benefits of budgeting is the ability to know when you can afford something and when you can't. It's great to be able to make a purchase without worrying whether you'll have enough for other needs.

In this lesson you will . . .
- **Learn how to use individual account sheets for each category to help you stay within your budget by category;**
- **Use a checking account;**
- **Learn how to integrate the individual account sheets with the checkbook ledger.**

Using individual account sheets is the key to this freedom.

If it were practical (and safe), you could hold all your money in cash, putting the prescribed amounts in different envelopes. Then, by looking in your "Miscellaneous" envelope, you would know whether you had an extra $239.95 for that new TV.

There's another way to accomplish the same thing: the use of individual account sheets.

STEP 1
Individual Account Sheets

You will need twelve copies of Form 3, "Individual Account Sheet"—one for each category except taxes and an additional one for your checkbook ledger.

Since it isn't safe to keep hundreds of dollars of cash in envelopes in your home, you will want to put most of each paycheck in the bank. You can then pay your bills by check—something we'll learn more about later in this lesson.

But first you need to know how to keep track of that money according to your budget categories. The idea of separate envelopes provides a good model. Think of each sheet as though it was an envelope containing the money you will need for that budget category this month. The money is "deposited" in an envelope for each category (housing, food, auto, etc.) and is then withdrawn as needed. The account sheets show you how much is there at any one time by recording how much is put in and how much is taken out. The total amount shown on all the account sheets equals the total amount in your checking account.

You should never spend based on your checking account balance. Spend by category, based on the individual account sheet. If your "Miscellaneous" individual account sheet says you have an extra $239.95, you can feel free to get that TV without worrying that you'll fall short somewhere else.

A. Study the examples below, which show typical activity on the individual account sheet for housing. They assume that NSI is $1,500 and that the housing allocation is $420.

First: Notice the information at the top: the name of the category—"Housing," the monthly allocation—$420, the amount applied to this category from the first period—$420, and the amount applied from the second pay period—$0.

Example:

INDIVIDUAL ACCOUNT SHEET			FORM 3
3 HOUSING ACCOUNT NAME	*$420.* MONTHLY ALLOCATION	*$420.* 1st PAY PERIOD	*−0−* 2nd PAY PERIOD

DATE		DEPOSIT	W/DRAW	BALANCE

The entire $420 allocation comes out of the first pay period in order to pay the mortgage near the beginning of the month. (This you determined during the last lesson, using Form 2, "Division of Pay.")

Second: In this example, assume that the first paycheck just arrived. Therefore, on the first line of the housing individual account sheet, notice the date (use 1-1 for January 1), the amount of the "deposit" into this category and the balance.

Example:

	INDIVIDUAL ACCOUNT SHEET		FORM 3

3 HOUSING	$420	$420	- 0 -
ACCOUNT NAME	MONTHLY ALLOCATION	1st PAY PERIOD	2nd PAY PERIOD

DATE		DEPOSIT	W/DRAW	BALANCE
1-1	DEPOSIT	$420.00		$420.00

This shows $420 available to spend on housing this month.

Third: As bills come due, they can be paid up to the $420 allotment. Each check is recorded on the appropriate individual account sheet along with the resulting balance.

Example:

	INDIVIDUAL ACCOUNT SHEET		FORM 3

3 HOUSING	$420	$420	- 0 -
ACCOUNT NAME	MONTHLY ALLOCATION	1st PAY PERIOD	2nd PAY PERIOD

DATE		DEPOSIT	W/DRAW	BALANCE
1-1	DEPOSIT	$420.00		$420.00
1-1	CK 102 NATIONAL Mortgage		$275.00	145.00
1-4	CK 105 Regional Power Co.		65.88	79.12
1-13	CK 110 Home Insurance Mutual		24.99	54.13
1-19	CK 119 Telephone		46.85	7.28
2-1	DEPOSIT	420.00		427.28
2-1	CK 127 NATIONAL Mortgage		275.00	152.28

Notice:

1. With the first pay period next month, you would make a new deposit to this category, and add that amount to the balance.
2. The housing category balance declines with every check. This shows exactly how much is left to spend, just as an envelope containing cash would do.
3. You will also be maintaining a checking account balance that will show how much is left in your total bank account.

The next example shows how Form 1, "Monthly Income and Expenses," was the source of information for filling out Form 2, "Division of Pay." This in turn tells you how much goes into each category's Individual Account Sheet (Form 3). Notice that while housing is all allotted with the first pay period, other categories such as food and auto receive deposits twice a month.

Example:

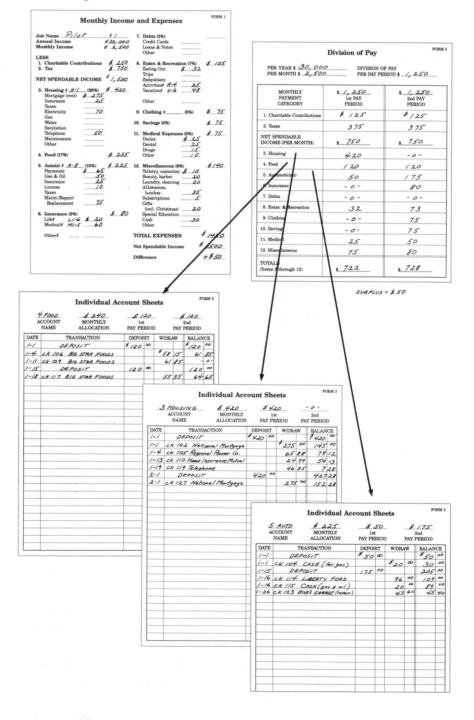

B. Now, fill out the top of a Form 3, "Individual Account Sheet," for each category, 1—12 (except for taxes). Write the amount of your initial deposit in each category. However, do not fill in the lines for payments yet. You will do that after you explore the fine points of keeping a checking account.

STEP 2
Using a Checking Account

So what's the big deal about using a checking account? In reality, about half of all check writers do not use their checking accounts properly. They make errors, can only guess at how much they have in their accounts, and are never able to balance their checkbook.

Many people pay overdraft charges of $10 per check (or more) and develop a very bad reputation with merchants who have been given bad checks.

Some people have been arrested for writing checks when they have insufficient funds to cover them. Even when legal prosecution doesn't ensue, the hassle and embarrassment is considerable. So it is a big deal, but it's not very complicated if you get started right.

Usually a bank checkbook will come with either a stub to write in the checks or a small ledger of its own. Since we can't provide you with an actual checkbook, use the Forms listed below to simulate your checkbook activity.

A. **Create your own checkbook ledger using a copy of Form 3, "Individual Account Sheet."** In the account name blank write, "Checkbook Ledger."

B. **Make a deposit of your imaginary paycheck every two weeks as shown with your Job Assignment.** Use the "Bank Deposits," Form 4, for this purpose. Notice that each paycheck equals half your monthly salary minus deductions (taxes).

C. **On your "Checkbook Ledger" enter the amount of each paycheck in the blanks for the first and second pay period. Add those two amounts together and enter the total in the blank above the monthly allocation.** This will be the total amount you have to work with for that month.

D. **For personal checks, you need ten copies of Form 5, "Blank Checks"—providing you with a total of thirty checks. Number each check sequentially, starting with #100.**

The example below shows a checkbook ledger for one month's records with two $875 paychecks. Each deposit and withdrawal is recorded and the balance maintained. (It does not include the check-writing charges which will be discussed in the next lesson.)

Example:

Individual Account Sheets   FORM 3

CHECKBOOK LEDGER	$1,750	$875	$875
ACCOUNT NAME	MONTHLY ALLOCATION	1st PAY PERIOD	2nd PAY PERIOD

DATE	CK#	TRANSACTION	DEPOSIT		W/DRAW		BALANCE	
1-1		DEPOSIT	875	00			875	00
1-1	101	FIRST CHURCH ①			125	00	750	00
1-1	102	NATIONAL MORTGAGE ③			275	00	475	00
1-1	103	CASH (E&R) ⑧			20	00	455	00
1-1	104	CASH (GAS) ⑤			20	00	435	00
1-4	105	REGIONAL POWER Co ③			65	88	369	12
1-4	106	BIG STAR FOODS ④			58	15	310	97
1-6	107	FAMILY ACTIVITY CENTER ⑧			25	00	285	97
1-8	108	SPARKLING CLEANERS ⑫			19	55	266	42
1-11	109	BIG STAR FOODS ④			61	85	204	57
1-13	110	HOME INS. MUTUAL ③			24	99	179	58
1-13	111	DR. GRABER (GLASSES) ⑪			68	13	111	45
1-13	112	CASH (LUNCHES) ⑫			40	00	71	45
1-15		DEPOSIT	875	00			946	45
1-15	113	FIRST CHURCH ①			125	00	821	45
1-16	114	LIBERTY FORD ⑤			96	00	725	45
1-16	115	CASH (GAS & OIL) ⑤			20	00	705	45
1-17	116	MED. INSURANCE ⑥			79	82	625	63
1-18	117	BIG STAR FOODS ④			55	35	569	28
1-20	118	THE EMBERS (MEAL OUT) ⑧			32	60	537	68
1-21	119	TELEPHONE ③			46	85	490	83
1-21	120	THE GAP (BLAZER) ⑨			73	26	417	57
1-25	121	BIG STAR FOODS ④			64	65	352	92
1-25	122	CASH (E&R) ⑧			20	00	332	92
1-26	123	BOB'S GARAGE (REPAIR) ⑤			43	60	289	32

STEP 3
Integrating Account Sheets and Checkbook Ledger

A. **Keep in mind that you're maintaining two separate records:** One (the checkbook ledger) tells you the total amount you have in your checking account.

The other (the individual account sheets) tells you how much is left in each category of your budget.

When you write a check, it must be posted (recorded) in both the checkbook ledger and the proper individual account sheet.

Although the example on the previous page shows $289.32 in the checking account, the checkbook ledger cannot be used to decide whether there is enough money to buy that $239.95 TV set. The individual account sheets tell you whether there is money available to meet some bills later.

Example:

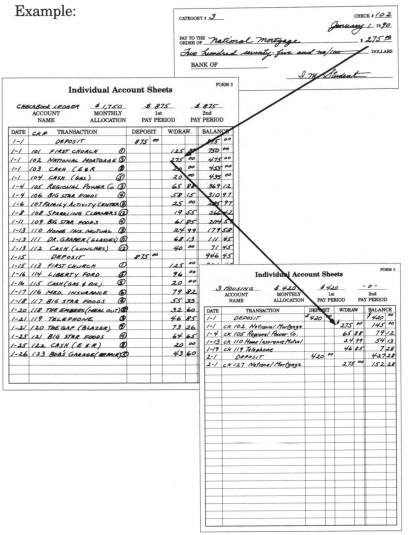

B. **Study this example.** It shows that on 1-1 (January 1) a deposit and four checks were recorded in the checkbook ledger. The deposit ($875) was divided among the various categories as predetermined on Form 2, "Division of Pay," from lesson 2.

Check #101 was recorded on the individual account sheet for charitable giving (category 1). Then, it was also recorded in the checkbook ledger, along with a circled (1) written next to the transaction to show that the individual account sheet for that category has been updated.

Similarly, check #102 was recorded on the housing individual account sheet (category 3), and a circled (3) was written in the checkbook ledger. Each check is recorded on the proper individual account sheet.

After updating all the categories, the total of the remaining funds in all categories on all the individual account sheets must equal the balance in the checkbook ledger.

STEP 4
Putting It into Practice

In Step 1 you should have filled out the heading on eleven individual account sheets—one for each category except taxes. If you have not done that, do it now.

You also should have filled out the heading of another individual account sheet as your checkbook ledger.

Now do the following steps to start this month's records:

A. Fill out a "Bank Deposit" slip (Form 4) for one paycheck.

B. Record that deposit in your checkbook ledger. Be sure to include the date and balance.

C. Divide that amount into categories by entering a "deposit" for each category on your individual account sheets. Each category receives its percentage of the total deposit.

D. Write one check each for categories 1 (if you are going to give anything away), 3, 4 (one fourth of your monthly food allocation), 8, and 9. Make up the names of the companies receiving payment. For instance, "National Mortgage" for a housing mortgage payment, "Big Star Foods" for your grocery store. See Appendix E.

E. Record all your checks in your checkbook ledger and calculate the running balances. Subtract the check amounts from the total deposit.

F. Record all your payments on the individual account sheets. Subtract the payments from the deposits.

G. Add up all the balances from your individual account sheets, and compare the figure to your checkbook ledger balance. If the amounts are the same, congratulations. Otherwise, review your calculations to locate your error.

This Is Your Life

Applying what you learn to your present finances.

1. Two weeks down—two weeks to go! Continue recording in your personal notebook all money in (income) and all money out (expenditures) for one month.

2. Use your "personalized" copy of Form 1, with the list you made of real spending categories (Food, Fun, Clothes, etc.), to estimate what percentage of your Net Spendable Income (NSI) you'd like to spend in each category. Remember, the total percentages must add up to 100 percent. Now calculate what amount of your NSI each percentage would be.

3. Using extra copies of Form 3, "Individual Account Sheets," fill in the name of each real spending category (one category per sheet). Save for use later.

4. Is your monthly income over $100? If so, consider opening a checking account. Keep a portion of your income as cash for miscellaneous expenses; pay for others (such as clothes) with a check.

BALANCING A CHECKING ACCOUNT

GETTING STARTED

By this time you have learned most of the basic steps in designing and keeping a budget. The previous lesson covered several of the most critical steps in record keeping. If you have any question about how to—

- make and record deposits,
- allocate funds to various accounts,
- write checks,
- balance a ledger, and
- record and balance expenditures in the individual account sheets,

then you should review those tasks from the last lesson.

In this lesson you will . . .
- **Conduct one month's worth of "business," simulating deposits, writing checks, and keeping double-entry records;**
- **Record the cost of checks and bank service charges;**
- **Reconcile your checkbook balance with your bank statement;**
- **Maintain a second month of budgeting (See "For Additional Study").**

STEP 1
Completing One Month of "Business"

Using Form 1, your "Monthly Income and Expense" sheet, and Form 2, your "Division of Pay" sheet, simulate a complete month of income and outflow of funds.

You have already deposited your first pay period in the bank. You allocated "deposits" of the appropriate amounts to the various categories (recorded on the individual account sheets). You have also made several first payments.

    A. **Continue the process, writing checks for all likely expenses in the first half of the month as designated by your "Division of Pay" sheet.** Make up logical dates, and create imaginary names for the companies or persons with whom you do business.

Include all undesignated categories like food, clothing, entertainment, recreation and miscellaneous. Make up imaginary purchases in amounts that are within each category's budgeted amount.

B. When you have completed this for the first half of the month, make a second paycheck deposit for January 15 (1-15). Proceed to fill out the expenses for the remainder of the month.

Your checkbook ledger should look similar to the sample ledger illustrated in Step 2 of the previous lesson. Of course, you will have used different names and amounts.

C. Record all expenditures in their corresponding individual account sheet. Put the circled number of the category on the checkbook ledger to show that you have recorded it.

The only individual account sheet categories that can legitimately not show any expenditures are:

1—Charitable Giving (if you chose to not give any away),

7—Debts (since you shouldn't have any), and

All other categories should list expenditures approaching your budgeted monthly allotment. If this is not the case, you may be overlooking some bill, and you certainly wouldn't want your refrigerator to become empty, your electricity turned off, or your car repossessed, etc.!

STEP 2
Catching Errors Before They Catch You

Once you record your month of "business", there are four important steps to make sure you have not made any errors. It is vital that you find errors before you try to spend money that you really may not have.

A. Add all the balances from the various categories of your individual account sheets.

B. Compare that total with the balance at the end of your checkbook ledger.

C. If they are not equal, go back over your work and find the error. Your error could be arithmetic or you might have forgotten to record some transaction in an appropriate place.

If your error was a failure to record something, you do not have to erase all your work. Simply record the missed transaction at the bottom of the others on the sheet. The date will show that it is out of order.

D. **Check again to see that everything balances.** This method of double-entry record keeping may seem tedious, but it is the only way to catch errors—which everyone inevitably makes from time to time. The point is to catch them before they lead you into an overdraft in your bank account.

STEP 3
Calculating Check Service Fees

In a future lesson we will evaluate the benefits of various checking account options. We will compare those accounts which offer free checking for preserving a minimum balance in your account against those that charge a fee for each check.

However, for our present purposes, we will assume that your account charges a ten-cent fee for each check that you write.

Some checkbook ledgers provide a method for adding that fee to the amount of each check. However, it is easier to add a total amount at the end of the month...provided you never reduce your account so low that the fees would put you into the red.

The way to calculate the fees at the end of the month is simply count the number of checks you wrote that month, multiply the amount by ten cents (or whatever your per-check fee happens to be), and subtract that amount from your balance on your checkbook ledger.

A. **Subtract your check-writing fees for the month you have just recorded.** Use ten cents per check as the fee.

In your checkbook ledger, write the date and the reason for the entry on the transaction part of the line. Put the total amount in the withdrawal column, and recalculate your balance.

B. **Record this charge on your individual account sheet under "miscellaneous."** It's an expense you need to account for just like anything else.

STEP 4
Reconciling Your Checkbook Ledger and Bank Statement

Each month your bank will send you a statement of your account. The statement shows your deposits, your withdrawals (checks they have processed), your fees, and the balance.

The bank statement lets you check your financial record keeping. However, do not rely on it to replace careful record keeping of your own. By the time you find out from your bank that you

FOR ADDITIONAL STUDY

1. Why is it important to do double-entry record keeping? Find two people who keep budgets, at least one of whom uses some form of a double-entry system. Ask both of them whether they have ever made any errors. How did they find their errors? How long has it usually taken them to find their errors? What might have happened if they had not found them?

2. Carry over your balances from your "January" records and do a second month of budget keeping. Refer to the Monthly Expenses "For Month #2" in Appendix E.

forgot to enter some expenditure or made a $100 error in subtraction, you could be in serious trouble.

In this study there is no way to provide an "outside" bank statement, so you must do the following on Form 6, "Checking Account Reconciliation:"

A. **Add up all your deposits** (from your deposit slips, not your ledger).

B. **Add up all the checks you have written.** (Use your actual checks, not your ledger.)

C. **Subtract B from A.**

D. **Multiply the number of checks you have written by ten cents. Subtract D from C to find your Bank Balance.**

The Bank Balance should be the same as your checkbook ledger balance.

E. **If the figures do not agree, find your error.**

In real life, your bank balance will not include some of the most recent checks you have written since they may not have been processed yet. Your last deposit will not show if it was made after the end of the bank's accounting period. Most bank statements have a work area and instructions for incorporating the unprocessed transactions into the bank's balance. By following this procedure you will come up with a new balance which should match your personal ledger.

If these amounts do not balance, search for the error. If you cannot find it or believe it to be the bank's mistake, contact the bank to resolve the difference. Don't just ignore the problem. These figures need to agree to the penny. And in the end, it will be the amounts the bank uses that matter.

This Is Your Life

Applying what you learn to your present finances.

1. Home stretch! Keep that running list of income and outgo up to date!

2. If you have a checking account, be sure you keep a running balance by subtracting each check written from the total. When your monthly bank statement arrives, be sure to reconcile what it says with what your checkbook says.

LOANS AND CREDIT CARDS

GETTING STARTED

B y this point in the course you should have
- two months of income and expenses budgeted,
- all your bills paid for those months, and
- money reserved for the irregular expenses that come up less often than once a month.

If your budget, individual account sheets, checkbook ledger, and bank statement all balance, you are doing great. You can skip the rest of this Getting Started section.

If your records are not in balance, you should go back and work on them until they do. You may need to seek help to find the problem and resolve it. Listed below are the basic budgeting steps that we have covered.

In this lesson, you will . . .
- **Discover how interest rates are calculated;**
- **Compare the difference between "simple interest" and "add-on interest;"**
- **Consider some of the dangers in borrowing money;**
- **Receive some tips on borrowing and using credit cards;**
- **Maintain your budget for a third month (see "For Additional Study").**

If necessary, start back at Lesson 1, Step 1 and redo the whole process until your records are all in balance:

1. Select a job from Appendix A. On Form 1, "Monthly Income and Expenses," enter your job number, your title, your annual income, and monthly income.
2. Determine your NSI (Net Spendable Income) by subtracting your charitable giving and taxes from your monthly income. Enter your NSI on Form 1.
3. Calculate your category limits on Form 1. Do this by multiplying the category percentage by your NSI. Your percentages cannot exceed 100 percent, and the total dollar amount of your category limits cannot exceed your NSI.
4. Select your budget needs from Appendix B for each category. The actual amount should not exceed the limits you have set for each category. List the dollar amounts for each category on Form 1.

5. Make sure income and expenses balance on Form 1.
6. Using Form 2, "Division of Pay," divide your expenses per pay period.
7. Using Form 3, "Individual Account Sheet," set up your budget system. Use one sheet for each category (charitable contributions, housing, auto, etc.).
8. Using Form 3, start a checking account ledger.
9. For at least one full month: record your deposits from your paycheck on the "Bank Deposits" slips, Form 4. Record your deposits in your checkbook ledger and each category's individual account sheet. Write checks (from Form 5, "Blank Checks") for all expenses and record those expenditures in your checkbook ledger and on the corresponding individual account sheet.
10. Balance your checkbook ledger, your budget, and your bank statement.

If your budget doesn't balance but you have not made any errors in your arithmetic, then your problem may be that you are spending more than you are earning. This is an all-too-common problem and causes many people more problems than they realize.

Which brings us to the subject of this lesson: loans. When faced with a cash problem, many people take out a loan. When their bills amount to more than their income, they resort to a "consolidation loan." This means that they take out a loan to cover all their other debts. However, the consolidation loan is often only a "stopgap" measure unless they also change their spending patterns. In any case, the cost of borrowing is always greater than what they would have paid in cash.

STEP 1
Understanding Interest Rates
A. Simple Interest

When you borrow money, the lender expects to make a profit. It's his or her money, and you are just "renting it." The way the lender "collects rent" is by charging interest, the fee for using another person's money.

However, the way the interest is calculated and whether it is fixed or variable can make a big difference in how much you ultimately pay.

Several years ago a law was passed by the United States Congress called "The Truth in Lending Act." It requires that all interest be stated by its APR (Annualized Percentage Rate). This means how it would compare with a "simple" interest loan.

A simple interest loan means that the interest you pay is calculated each month on the unpaid balance. For example, let's assume you borrowed $1,000 at 12 percent annual interest to be paid back in ten monthly installments. The 12 percent annual interest is the same as 1 percent interest per month. Therefore, the payments would be calculated approximately as follows:

First payment:	1/10 of initial loan ($1,000)	=	$100
	Plus 1% interest on balance	=	10
	Payment	=	$110
Balance of loan = **$900**			
Second payment:	1/10 of initial loan ($1,000)	=	$100
	Plus 1% interest on balance	=	9
	Payment	=	$109
Balance of loan = **$800**			
Third payment:	1/10 of initial loan ($1,000)	=	$100
	Plus 1% interest on balance	=	8
	Payment	=	$108
Balance of loan = **$700**			
Fourth payment:	1/10 of initial loan ($1,000)	=	$100
	Plus 1% interest on balance	=	7
	Payment	=	$107
Balance of loan = **$600**			
Etc.			

In reality, the actual figures do not break down so neatly in even dollar amounts. The total payments, including interest, would be added together and then divided by ten so that each monthly payment would be equal—in this case $105.58 per month. The total amount of interest would be $55.80.

The graph below depicts how simple interest works in a $1000 loan at 12 percent interest for ten months. At any time you elect to pay the loan off, you would save the remaining interest.

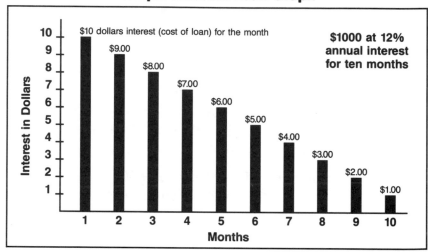

Simple Interest Loan Graph

B. Add-On Interest

Before the "Truth in Lending Act," if you financed a loan at 12 percent "add-on interest," you would have received a big shock. Because "add-on" interest is calculated over the length of the loan (ten months in our example) and not on the unpaid balance each month. Also the payment schedule is designed so that much of the interest is paid up front. The disadvantage of this is that if you wanted to pay your loan off early, say at the end of four months on a ten-month loan, you would save little or no interest.

On the ten-month simple interest loan shown earlier, your total interest would be about $55. On the same loan at a 12 percent add-on rate, the total interest would be nearly $100 or an annual percentage rate (APR) of more than 21 percent! Without a doubt, you always need to know the APR on any loan.

The graph below clearly shows how the interest on an add-on loan, paid in any certain month, is much greater than that of a simple interest loan paid off in the same month.

Add-on Interest Loan Graph

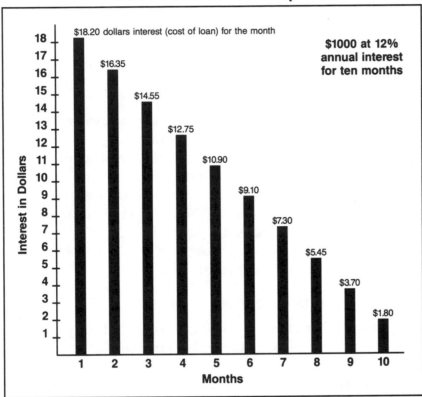

$18.20 dollars interest (cost of loan) for the month

$1000 at 12% annual interest for ten months

$16.35
$14.55
$12.75
$10.90
$9.10
$7.30
$5.45
$3.70
$1.80

Interest in Dollars

Months

For long-term loans on purchases such as cars, it would always be wiser to negotiate a simple interest loan. Then if you were able to pay it off early, you would save on the remaining interest.

STEP 2
The Dangers of Living on Borrowed Money

It has become increasingly popular in our society to live on borrowed money. The government does it, many businesses do it, and so do many individuals.

So why not live on borrowed money?

1. Borrowing is expensive.

The money you pay in interest can always be used better for other purposes.

Let's suppose you took out a $1,000 loan at 15 percent interest to buy a new living room set. You arrange to pay it back over a

three-year period at about $35 per month. Your costs would look like this:

The store price of the purchase	$1,000
The amount of interest over three years	248
TOTAL OUTLAY	$1,248

Most of us can think of better things to do with $248.

2. Borrowing is addictive.

When your money is going to pay for past debts, you cannot use it to meet current needs. Not only do you lose your freedom of choice, but you are tempted to borrow more money as the only seeming solution when you encounter unforeseen expenses.

Let's say your car breaks down and the repair costs $150. You may feel forced to borrow again. Whereas, if you had been saving for that living room set instead of paying for it on time, you would at least have the choice of using some of that money for the car repair and postponing the furniture.

3. Borrowing is deceptive.

Why do you think merchants will go through all the paperwork of credit card sales plus pay the credit card company a percentage of every sale?

The reason is that research has shown that people will spend as much as 20 percent more when shopping on credit as over shopping with cash. Somehow it is easier to buy now and pay later. Apparently, when the average person has to put down cold, hard cash in order to make a purchase, they are more careful.

Most of us need to be more conservative shoppers.

STEP 3
Tips for Using Credit or Borrowing Money

Nonetheless, there may come times when you need to borrow money or use a credit card. When you do, here are some guidelines.

1. Never borrow money needlessly. For instance, never borrow money to purchase an ego trip. Never borrow for an impulse purchase. Wait to consider it.
2. Remember that you will always have to pay for what you borrow. Even if you should go bankrupt, you'll pay in years of bad reputation, no credit, inconvenience, and other painful losses.
3. Make certain that the benefits of borrowing far exceed the cost

of the loan liability and the restrictions placed on your future by the burden of repayment.

4. Make certain that your purchase will last longer than it takes to pay for it. It is a good goal never to purchase a depreciable (declining in value) item on credit. A car is a prime example of a depreciable item, since the value of most cars drops substantially the minute you sign your name to the sales agreement. (Lesson 8 deals with buying a car.)

5. Your goal should be to use your credit cards only if you can pay off the entire amount by the due date. Credit card interest is terribly high. If you can't control your credit card use, destroy them.

6. If you experience a problem making payments, go immediately to your creditor. Explain the situation and work out an agreeable arrangement. Do everything you can to save your credit rating.

7. Never loan out your credit cards to anyone you wouldn't allow free access to your cash. If a credit card is lost or stolen, report it immediately to limit your liability.

ONE BIG BORROWING DECISION

Many young people and their families face a major decision about borrowing if the young person wants to attend college. In a high percentage of cases, borrowing money seems to be the only way to pay for the high costs of education. Borrowing for college is more logical than borrowing to buy a car because a good education increases your earning capabilities. Thus, it is an appreciating item, while a car depreciates in value.

However, borrowing for college is still a loan that carries significant obligations and risks. Many young people who borrow to attend school find it extremely difficult to start their careers and their homes because of the heavy load of debt they have assumed. Because of their debt, they never have enough money available for the things they want and need, and so they continue to borrow, increasing their living costs and locking themselves into a long-term life of financial pressure.

Before borrowing money to pay for college, look for alternatives. Consider attending a community or junior college for the first year or two, then transfer to a more expensive four-year college or university. Look into employment opportunities which may allow you to work for a year or two and save enough to pay for many school expenses. Evaluate the costs of attending a nearby school and living at home instead of going away to college. Explore the work programs provided by employers who will help employees go to college. Weigh the benefits of enlisting in the military before entering college. Investigate the scholarships and grants which are available, many of which go unclaimed because students would rather borrow and not have to work.

SAVINGS AND INVESTMENT: KEYS TO AVOIDING DEBT

There's really only one way to avoid debt: discipline yourself not to go into debt. A big part of this discipline is to make a budget which balances income and outgo. Part of this budget must involve designating a portion of your regular income for savings and investments. Only by following this pattern will you be able to deal with added, unexpected expenses without borrowing.

Here are five tips for developing a good savings and investment strategy:

1. Set Clear-Cut Investment Goals
Saving money without a purpose is hoarding and leads to no beneficial result. It is wise to set aside money for specific future needs: education, buying a home or car, vacation, retirement, etc. It is also wise to set aside a portion of savings in case of unexpected expenses.

2. Evaluate Risk and Return
To earn an increase on any investment, there is a degree of risk. The guideline is: the higher the rate of return, the higher the risk. If you find an investment that promises a high rate of return but advertises a low degree of risk, watch out; there's no free lunch. If you can't afford to lose it, play it safe with a low-risk investment.

3. Be Patient
A smart investor will keep some cash on hand for emergencies. As a general rule though, only about 5 to 10 percent of your savings should be in cash or near-cash type investments. These include savings accounts, bonds, certificates of deposit, treasury bills and money market funds. Other investments should get your money working for you as long as you are patient and do not expect to get rich quick.

4. Diversify
There's an old saying, ''Don't put all your eggs in one basket.'' That certainly applies to your investment strategy. Let's assume you have $500 to invest. If you buy stock in one company, then all of your money rests on how that one company does. One effective alternative is called a mutual fund. In a mutual fund your money is pooled with many others' and invested in a variety of different companies. Look for a mutual fund which invests in different areas of the economy (real estate, gold and silver, stocks and bonds, etc.), thus helping to cushion against declines in specific areas.

5. Take a Long-Range View
The vast majority of investors tend to panic when their investments start to lose money. As a result, they often pull out when they should have stayed in. A stable, diversified investment plan will help you ride out short-term downturns.

This Is Your Life

Applying what you learn to your present finances.

1. Congratulations on keeping track of your money for a whole month! Use this record to do the following:

   a. Total up your income; total your expenditures (plus any money you have left over). How do the actual totals compare to your estimated monthly income and estimated Net Spendable Income?

   b. Now list each of your expenditures from the past month under one of the categories you created on the "Individual

Account Sheets" (Form 3). (For example: List the $3.40 for pizza and $5.39 at McDonald's under the Food category. List the $9.80 you spent for gas under Transportation; etc.) Add up the expenses in each category; figure what percentage each total is of your NSI. How do your actual amounts and percentages for each category compare to the estimated budget you figured out earlier? (See "This Is Your Life," Lesson 3, #3.)

c. Do you like what you see? Were your earlier estimated percentages and amounts realistic? Is too much going for pizza and bowling and not enough for clothes? Using the record of your actual income and expenses for one month, make a budget for next month. What percentage of your NSI do you want to allot to each category? Calculate what that percentage would be in actual dollars.

d. Using the budget you have just created, begin keeping a record of actual income and expenses once again. This time, however, record each expenditure under its proper category and deduct it from the amount you have budgeted for it this month. Try to remain within the amounts allotted.

2. Have you recently borrowed money from your parents? a friend? the bank? How are you paying it back—a portion each month? in one lump sum? Are you paying interest? If so, figure how much you will pay altogether. Do you have to borrow money often? Can you think of another way to plan for those expenses?

3. What is your plan for saving? What are your savings goals?

FOR ADDITIONAL STUDY

Carry over your balances from your "February" records and do a third month of budget keeping, following the third month of examples in Appendix E. You will find that doing another month of calculations this week will make the process easier and the errors will probably diminish.

Take the following quiz to review the main ideas of this session.

1. True or False—Simple interest means you don't have to qualify to get a loan.

2. True or False—Add-on interest means that the interest you pay is added back onto the loan.

3. True or False—The "Truth in Lending Act" requires that all interest be stated as an Annualized Percentage Rate.

4. The method of calculating interest by law is the:
   A. Awful Percentage Rate.
   B. The Discount Rate.
   C. The Annualized Percentage Rate.
   D. The Prime Rate.

5. The best type of loan rate is:
   A. Usury.
   B. Compound.
   C. Add-on.
   D. Simple.

COPING WITH BUDGET BUSTERS

GETTING STARTED

It would be great if budgeting in real life were merely a matter of keeping track of your income and planned expenses each month. Unfortunately, unplanned expenses do occur and they must be paid.

You will receive one of these budget busters during this lesson. This new expense will show that budgeting is a dynamic process. Your budget is not a straitjacket. It's your tool to help you manage your money. Therefore, when unexpected variables arise, your budget needs to change to meet your needs.

In this lesson, you will . . .
- **Face a typical budget problem and learn how to cope;**
- **Discover some of the most common checking account options available and learn their advantages and disadvantages;**
- **Maintain your budget for a fourth month.**

STEP 1
A "Budget Buster"

The following example shows how a "budget buster" could be handled.

Suppose you have a $30,000 per year income and have completed one month of record keeping. Your budget buster is an auto accident for which you were at fault. You have a fine of $35 to pay and car repairs of $1,500. Your insurance has a $100 deductible. (You must pay the first $100 of any claim.) Let's also suppose that you have $45.40 remaining in your auto account but only $31.40 of that can be used for repairs. The rest must be saved for license and insurance.

Both the fine and the deductible must be worked into your budget. (It is times like this when those expensive insurance premiums are worth it!)

(The example below shows only how funds are transferred from one account to another. It does not show all the other transactions that would have taken place in these categories by this time in the month.)

Example:

To pay $35 traffic fine.

INDIVIDUAL ACCOUNT SHEET FORM 3

12 Miscellaneous *$155* *$75* *$80*

ACCOUNT NAME	MONTHLY ALLOCATION	1st PAY PERIOD	2nd PAY PERIOD

DATE		DEPOSIT	W/DRAW	BALANCE
	(amount remaining in account)			*$99.55*
1-29	*Ck 124 Traffic Fine*		*$35.00*	*64.55*

Transfer funds to allow Auto to pay deductible.

INDIVIDUAL ACCOUNT SHEET FORM 3

10 Savings *$75* *–0–* *$75*

ACCOUNT NAME	MONTHLY ALLOCATION	1st PAY PERIOD	2nd PAY PERIOD

DATE		DEPOSIT	W/DRAW	BALANCE
	(amount remaining in account)			*75.00*
1-31	*Transfer to Auto ⑤*		*68.60*	*6.40*

Payment of deductible.

INDIVIDUAL ACCOUNT SHEET FORM 3

5 Auto *$225* *$50* *$175*

ACCOUNT NAME	MONTHLY ALLOCATION	1st PAY PERIOD	2nd PAY PERIOD

DATE		DEPOSIT	W/DRAW	BALANCE
	(amount remaining in account)			*45.40*
1-30	*Deposit (Transfer from Savings ⑩)*	*68.60*		*114.00*
1-31	*Ck 125 Auto Repair*		*100.00*	*14.00*

Note: The traffic fine was paid out of Category 12, "Miscellaneous." The deductible amount for the repairs ($100) was paid out of Category 5, "Auto." ($31.40 was there already plus a transfer of $68.60 from Category 10, "Savings"). In this case, there was enough surplus in savings to cover the expense, so a loan was unnecessary.

A. **Now turn to Appendix C, "Budget Busters," in the back of this book. There you will find your personal "budget buster."**

1. If your annual income is below $25,500, and you have completed one or two months of record keeping, you have just been hit by "Budget Buster A."

2. If it is above $25,500, and you have completed one or two months of record keeping, you have just been hit by "Budget Buster B."

3. If it is below $25,500, and you have completed three months of budgeting, you have just been hit by "Budget Buster C."

4. If it is above $25,500, and you have completed three months of budgeting, you have just been hit by "Budget Buster D."

If you are taking this course as a class, your teacher may assign you a different budget buster.

B. **Your job is to adjust your budget to cover this expense.** Make these adjustments on the end of the last month you have completed. To do this you may need to dip into your savings.

STEP 2
Taking Out a Loan

If you have an expense greater than what that budget category plus your savings can cover, you must take out a loan, following actions A—D below.

If you do not need a loan, read through these steps anyway so you can see the impact of a loan on your budget, then continue with Step 3 of this lesson.

A. **In Appendix D, "Loan Table," find the amount you need to borrow.** For the purposes of this study, select the $100 amount equal to or just above what you need. Then find the corresponding monthly payments necessary to repay the loan in three years at 12 percent interest (APR).

B. **Make out a new copy of Form 1, "Monthly Income and Expenses." Incorporate your loan repayment under Category 7, "Debts."** Then adjust your other categories so that your total percentages do not exceed 100 percent and your total dollar amount does not exceed your NSI.

C. **Fill out Form 7, the "Loan Application."**

D. **If you are working in class or with someone else, obtain "approval" from your leader or partner for your loan.**

Approval of your loan should be based upon whether you have calculated your monthly payments accurately and have come up with a balanced and reasonable new "Monthly Income and Expenses" form.

Evaluating Checking Account Options

Another variable for your budget is the type of checking account you use. There are many options available for checking accounts. **Study the following three common options and make note of each one's advantages and potential problems:**

Minimum deposit checking.

Most banks, savings and loans, etc., offer no-fee checking for customers who maintain an average minimum balance in their accounts, usually $500 or more. Otherwise one has to pay a fee for each check written, plus a minimum service charge per month.

In evaluating whether or not to leave a portion of your savings in a checking account that pays no interest so that you can keep your balance above the no-fee minimum, consider the cost versus the earnings.

For example: if a bank offered free checking with a minimum deposit of $500 or would pay you 6 percent interest (APR) on the money in savings, it might seem better to leave the money in savings. However, if you're charged 10 cents per check, plus a monthly service charge of $3.00 and you write thirty checks per month, that's $6.00 per month for checking. You would have to earn over 14 percent (APR) on your $500 to match the cost of checking. You're much better off financially to take advantage of their minimum deposit, free checking offer.

Automatic tellers.

Most banks offer automatic tellers for banking transactions after regular business hours. These can be a great convenience, but they can also be easily misused.

The most common problem associated with automatic tellers is withdrawing cash and not recording it in the checkbook ledger. This error gives the impression of more money in checking than is really there, often resulting in overdrawn accounts.

First, remember that any withdrawals should fit within your budget. If you take cash out because you have spent all your budgeted cash, you're robbing money that you'll need for something else later.

Second, all withdrawals must be recorded whether they are made by check, automatic teller, cashier, etc. When you use an automatic teller, make a regular habit of recording it as soon as you get home.

Automatic overdraft protection.

Many banks offer their checking account customers a service that will pay overdrawn checks rather than return them because of insufficient funds. This sounds great on the surface, but it leads to some very sad consequences.

Because they know their overdrawn checks are going to be paid, many people are tempted to overdraw their accounts regularly.

Also, this feature encourages those who don't like to balance their checkbook ledgers to be slothful and not do so because they feel it's not necessary.

Finally, overdrafts are charged to the customer's credit card account and interest is charged just as if the credit card had been used to obtain cash. Cash drawn on credit cards begins accumulating interest charges immediately and at the credit card's very high rate. This can lead to a lot of debt in a hurry.

At best, an automatic overdraft system encourages bad habits. At worst, it can lead to unmanageable debt. Remember, when you reach the debt limit, the bank will no longer honor the overdraft protection, so you'll be right back where you started, only deeply in debt as well. So it's better never to start using the overdraft protection in the first place.

This Is Your Life

Applying what you learn to your present finances.

1. Continue to record your expenditures on the "Individual Account Sheets" by category. Deduct from the amount you have allotted for each category as you go, so you can see at a glance what you have left to spend.
2. Think back: What unplanned expense (a real-life Budget Buster!) have you had to cope with in the last four months? (Dent in the car fender? Big date that cost more than you planned?) How did you cope with it: did your parents bail you out? have savings to cover? borrow and pay back?
3. Think ahead: Does your current budget allow some leeway for future unplanned expenses?
4. If you have a checking account, what checking account options are you using—free checking for minimum deposit? automatic teller privilege? overdraft protection? Have they helped or hindered you in "living within your means"?

FOR ADDITIONAL STUDY

Maintain your budget for another month, recording another month's worth of income and expenses. Follow the fourth month of examples in Appendix E. Be sure to incorporate the consequences of your budget-buster, especially if you had to take out a loan.

To review how you are grasping the ideas of this course so far, take the following quiz.

1. True or False—Avoiding checking account service charges can be more profitable than earning interest.
2. True or False—Automatic overdraft protection is a no-cost service offered by many banks.
3. True or False—Automatic tellers can be used for after-hours transactions.
4. The greatest problem with automatic tellers is:
   A. They talk too much.
   B. Other people getting your money.
   C. Unrecorded withdrawals.
   D. None of the above.
5. A service to guarantee overdrawn checks is:
   A. An automatic service charge.
   B. An automatic teller.
   C. An automatic debit.
   D. An automatic overdraft protection.

UNDERSTANDING INSURANCE

GETTING STARTED

Review your budget and see if it is still in balance after incorporating your budget-buster from the last lesson. If it is, congratulations! However, if it won't balance, you need to stop right here and get some help.

If you're taking this course in a group, then speak to your leader. If you are taking it on your own, then your parents are the first choice. If they can't help you, go to some other adult who can. It can be almost anyone, but a good resource might be a banker, accountant, high school economics teacher, etc.

If your budget simply has more expenses than income, you need to do some trading, eliminating or reducing some expenses.

In this lesson, you will . . .
- **Evaluate various types of life insurance;**
- **Select the amount and type of life insurance which is right for you;**
- **Maintain your budget for a fifth month. (See "For Additional Study.")**

STEP 1
Evaluating Life Insurance

The purpose of life insurance is to provide for someone you love after you die. Right now you probably don't have to concern yourself with that decision, but eventually you will. This study will help you make the decisions you'll face later in life. There are three basic questions to be asked (and answered) about life insurance:

1. How much do you need?
2. How much can you afford?
3. What kind is best?

These questions are best answered through an illustration.

Imagine a young family of four where the husband is the primary wage earner, making $24,000 a year.

1. How much insurance do they need?

The wage earner makes $24,000 per year. Social Security survivors' benefits would pay roughly $11,000 per year to his wife and children, leaving a deficit of $13,000 per year. Therefore, the death benefits (the money paid to the beneficiaries of the insurance policy) would need to be large enough to yield $13,000 per year. Assuming the money could be invested at 10 percent interest, a policy of $130,000 would be needed. ($13,000 is 10 percent of $130,000, or $13,000/year 10% = $130,000).

So now we know the answer to the first question. The husband should take out $130,000 worth of life insurance.

2. How much can they afford?

This can be answered by referring to the insurance category of their budget on Form 1, "Monthly Income and Expenses." Let's assume that the maximum amount they can afford is $15 of their NSI (net spendable income) per month.

3. What kind is best for them?

The kind of insurance that will be best for them can be determined by their need for a $130,000 policy and their available funds (a maximum of $15 per month). At age 24, this husband would have to buy "term" insurance.

STEP 2
Types of Insurance

Term insurance is the only choice where funds are severely limited. "Term" insurance means that it is purchased for a set period of time (one year, five years, ten years, etc.). At the end of the term, the policy can be renewed, but the cost goes up and generally will continue to do so. (It goes up because with increasing age the potential for death and therefore a claim on the policy increases.)

Whole-life insurance is more expensive initially, but it accumulates a cash reserve. Whole-life (also called cash-value insurance) means that it is purchased for the insured's lifetime (that's why it's called "whole-life"). It usually has a monthly or yearly fee that starts out higher than a term policy, but is not increased with age.

In most whole-life policies, the cash reserves belong to the insurance company. It is a cash reserve set aside to offset the increasing age of the insured. The cash reserves can be used by the policyholder to offset payments at a later time. The policyholder can also borrow against the cash value, but it becomes a debt (plus interest), reducing the payout if the insured dies.

Many policies also pay dividends (earnings) to the policyholder. The dividends belong to the policy owner and can be used to offset the policy's cost, to purchase more insurance or as a means of saving.

Comparing Term and Whole-Life Insurance

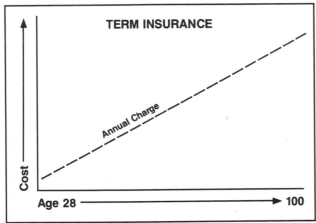

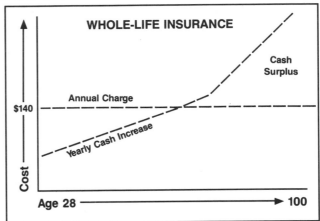

Since term insurance is always cheaper initially, it usually represents the best alternative for anyone with limited funds. In our example, this husband would have to buy term insurance because of the need for a $130,000 policy and only $15 a month is available to pay the premiums.

Be aware that the commission an insurance sales person receives on whole-life is much higher than on term insurance. Therefore, you can expect a stronger sales pitch for why you should buy whole-life—whether it is justified or not.

Paid-up insurance is a third type of policy. For this you invest a one-time, large sum of money to purchase coverage.

STEP 3
Selecting Life Insurance

When it is time to purchase life insurance, shop around before you purchase. Premiums can vary as much as 50 percent for equivalent coverage. **Study the following tips.**

The coverage you purchase is based on current mortality tables (the statistical averages of the ages at which people die). People's life expectancy keeps going up. The result should lower the cost of premiums (not considering inflation) because the average policy holder pays in longer.

The insurance you purchase should also take into account whether you are a smoker or not, since smoking severely reduces

life expectancy. Some companies recognize other health awareness or physical fitness programs in the policies they write. Try to buy life insurance through a group plan. You can save up to 40 percent, and medical exams are often waived.

Consider adjusting the amount of insurance you carry at significant stages in your life. When your family increases in size and your living expenses increase (larger house payments, etc.), you might increase your coverage so that your survivors could continue without undue hardship should you die.

On the other hand, when you get older, have paid off your home and your children are living on their own, you might reduce your coverage to match the actual financial obligations that continue rather than those you have already met.

However, if you have been paying for a whole-life policy for years, don't just drop it; see if you can convert it to some type of paid-up policy.

Now take Form 8, "Insurance Needs Worksheet," to calculate how much insurance you would need. Assume that you are the sole source of income for your household and that Social Security would provide $11,000 per year.

On the form, Line 3 equals your family's additional annual need. Line 4 is found by multiplying Line 3 by ten because we are assuming the life insurance settlement could be invested at 10 percent interest.

To determine the lump-sum costs, include the total amount of any debt you have plus $3,000 for funeral costs, and $40,000 for the college education of each child.

This Is Your Life

Applying what you learn to your present finances.

1. Two weeks of spending by your budget—how's it going? Have you overspent in one category and had to borrow from another? Just be sure to keep track of all expenses.
2. What kind of insurance—if any—do you need at this point in your life: auto; driver's; student; sports medical? Who is paying for it? What are the benefits? What is the monthly premium? If you don't know—find out!

BUYING CARS

GETTING STARTED

Virtually everyone faces the need to buy a car at one time or another. We're a mobile society, and even within large cities with public transportation systems, most people own cars.

The two largest purchases most people will make with their personal finances are houses and cars. It is important to know how and where to get the best deals. In this study, we'll concentrate on cars.

Granted, most people need a car, but in reality, cars represent a lot more than just transportation. For many people, a car expresses the image of who they think they are or would like to be. Thus, they are likely to spend excessively.

In this lesson, we're going to look at four decision areas: buying new cars, leasing cars, buying used cars, and financing.

In this lesson, you will . . .
- **Learn the pros and cons of buying a new car;**
- **Find out the real cost of leasing a car;**
- **Discover how to shop for a used car;**
- **Study the alternatives in financing a car;**
- **Maintain your budget for one final month (see "For Additional Study").**

STEP 1
Buying a New Car

There are few purchases that are more exciting than buying a new car, and an old car never seems so bad as when you begin looking at new ones. Unfortunately, most budgets cannot absorb the full cost of a new car. As a result, a common technique used in selling new cars is to de-emphasize the total cost and focus only on the monthly payments. These often are calculated based on the cheapest model over four to six years and often contain a "balloon" note as the last payment. Such a note can range from several hundred to thousands of dollars.

One advantage of purchasing a new car is that you can sometimes get a lower interest rate on a loan if you need to finance it. However, the depreciation on a new car is often as much as

25 percent of the purchase price as soon as the buyer signs the title papers. For example, when a new car is financed at 80 percent of the purchase price over forty-eight months, its resale value may not equal the amount owed until the last few months of the loan. Many new car buyers experience the shock of trying to sell a car, only to discover they owe several thousand dollars more than it's worth!

What a deal, huh?

However, if, after considering all the facts, you still decide to buy a new car, then you need to get the best car you can. The following steps can be helpful:

1. **Decide what type of car you need** (two-door, four-door, truck, etc.).
2. **Establish your maximum price range** (based on your budget).
3. **Decide what equipment you want** (air conditioning, automatic, power steering, etc.).
4. **Determine the make and model of car you want.** If you're willing to be totally objective, shop every make available. Give the salespeople your criteria and ask them for their best deal. It is usually best to shop without offering a trade-in. It's easier to compare prices without trade-in variables. Also, talk as if it is a cash transaction so that you can also remove the financing variable.
5. **Finally before buying, compare the best deals offered with a good, independent consumer products rating service** (such as *Consumer Reports* magazine). Determine which is the best quality car at the best price. Often the repair rating and insurance costs can mean a difference in practical value of hundreds or even thousands of dollars over the life of the car.

STEP 2
Leasing a Car

More and more, leasing has become a popular option for non-business car buyers. The motivation is usually the lack of an adequate down payment to buy a car outright. However, leasing is generally a more expensive way to drive a car as the following example from Consumer Reports magazine shows.

"The Numbers Game" (Footnote 1. From *Consumer Reports,* April 1988, p. 217. Reprinted by permission.)

The table below compares the cost of leasing a 1988 Toyota Camry with the cost of financing and the cost of buying with cash. The lease-or-buy decision is a close one in this example because the Camry has a good residual value. The deal you get will vary according to the type of car you want and how well you negotiate the different elements of the lease.

Up-front costs. To lease the car, you would have to pay a refund security deposit, usually equal to one month's lease payment. To buy the car with financing, you'd need a 20 percent down payment ($2,600), plus the sales tax. (We figured the sales tax at 5 percent, the national average.) Without financing you'd need to come up with $13,000 cash plus the sales tax.

Continuing costs. With a closed-end lease, you would make 48 monthly payments of $250, totaling $12,000. If you financed 80 percent of a purchase over four years at 10.5 percent, you would eventually pay out $10,400 in principal and $2,381 in interest. You would, however, be able to tax-deduct part of the interest on the loan. Result: net interest cost of $2,216.

Net opportunity cost. Any money invested up front results in the loss of interest that the money might otherwise have earned. This "opportunity cost" must be factored into the calculation. The opportunity cost is lowest for the lease, since you lose only the interest on your security deposit, and highest for the cash purchase.

In our example, we assumed you could have invested your money at 6.1 percent interest, a recent rate for money-market accounts. (If you think you can earn a higher return, use a higher amount when calculating the opportunity cost.) To find the net opportunity cost, we subtracted from the assumed interest earnings the income tax owed by someone in the 28 percent tax bracket.

Refunded security deposit. At the end of the lease, the one month's payment would be returned to you. You reduce the cost of the four-year lease by $250.

Residual value. The leased car has no value to you at the end of the lease. [You have to return it.] The owned car would still retain some value from the total cost of the purchase.

$13,000 Toyota Camry	Lease	Financed purchase	Cash purchase
Up-Front costs:			
Security deposit	$ 250	--	--
Down payment or cash	--	$ 2,600	$13,000
Sales tax	--	650	650
Continuing costs:			
Loan principal	--	10,400	--
Net interest expense	--	2,216	--
Closed-end lease	12,000	--	--
Net opportunity cost:	47	609	2,559
	$12,297	$16,475	$16,209
Less:			
Refunded security deposit	250	--	--
Residual value	--	5,000	5,000
Total four-year cost	$12,047	$11,475	$11,209

A lease agreement is as binding a contract as a loan. Failure to fulfill a lease is the same as defaulting on a loan. The car will be repossessed, you can be sued for any deficiencies, and your credit can be ruined. Also, very few people have the money to invest to take advantage of the "net opportunity cost." Therefore, the real cost of leasing or even financing a car is significantly higher for the average person! And how many people can pay cash for a new car?

STEP 3
Buying a Used Car

Most nonbusiness car buyers are better off selecting a good used car. Unfortunately, many people fear buying a used car because they're afraid they will get stuck with someone else's problem.

The truth is, most used cars less than three years old were traded because the owners got tired of them or they had relatively minor problems. That is not to say you can't get stuck with a defective used car. You can, just as you can get stuck with a defective new car. However, a little knowledge and caution can virtually eliminate that risk.

In buying a used car, go through the same criteria that was given for a new car. Once you know what you want and you locate several possible buys, go to the library and check out the cars in back issues of the consumer magazines.

Many used cars have transferable warranties that are assumable by second or even third buyers, so you will want to check out that possibility, also.

But from whom should you buy a used car?

The most common place to buy a used car is from **a used car dealer.** An honest, ethical dealer offers many advantages, such as a service department, limited warranties, an evaluation period, etc. However, often the best buys are found elsewhere.

Friends and relatives often have good used cars for sale and will make you a good deal. In addition, you can ask about the repair history of the car. However, if problems occur, a significant strain on the relationship may develop.

Newspaper ads are a popular way to locate people trying to sell their own cars. By buying direct, so to speak, you can usually get a lower price and may get a better history on the car. In most states, you also don't have to pay sales taxes on purchases from private individuals.

Car auctions are used by many car dealers to sell used cars taken as trade-ins. Most auctions are open to the public but require a bond or cash guarantee before you are allowed to bid on a car. In general, auctions are not the place for novice car buyers to purchase cars. The prices are usually great, but it is virtually impossible to know the history of the vehicle.

Now use Form 9, the "Car Selection Worksheet," and go through the exercise of selecting a car.

A. Locate several copies of recent, local newspaper car ads.

B. Secure a copy of a consumer products service that rates cars.

C. Find out what insurance will cost for several different cars. (This type of information is usually available at your local library.)

D. Look at your budget.
- Do you have any money saved for a down payment?
- How much can you afford to pay each month?
- Don't forget to leave room for the insurance and operating costs.

STEP 4
Financing a Car

At best, financing a car can be a bad deal, since the car is rarely worth what is owed on it. It is always better to save your money and buy what you can pay for with cash.

However, most young car buyers do finance at least a portion of their first car. If you must finance a car, here are some things you ought to know.

Low-interest loans. From time to time, car manufacturers will offer low-interest loans on new cars. However, there's an old cliche that says, "There are no free lunches." If you're offered a low-interest loan, there is always a reason. Usually you will pay a higher price for the car than you would if you arranged your own financing and dealt with the dealer on a cash-purchase basis. Sometimes only certain models (usually the most expensive and fully equipped) qualify for the low-interest loan. In the end, you pay more than you intended.

Dealer-arranged financing. Many dealers will offer to arrange financing for you. This often complicates the sale and makes the actual sales price difficult to determine. You may be able to get a lower interest rate by checking with several lenders (banks) of your own choosing or possibly the credit union at your work.

Collateral substitute. Because cars depreciate so rapidly, many lenders consider them a high-risk loan. Therefore, they carry a high interest rate. If you can provide alternative collateral for the loan, such as stocks, bonds, real-estate, etc., you can usually reduce the interest rate on the loan. If you don't have other collateral, perhaps a parent or relative does, and would be willing to use it. Warning: If the loan is not repaid, the substitute collateral can be lost.

A. **Estimate the finance charges you would be likely to pay if you secured a loan on several of the cars you investigated in Step 3.** Secure information on typical finance costs for used cars.

B. **Determine a reasonable down payment you can make from your savings** (keeping in mind that you will be looking to buy or rent a home in the next session).

C. **Determine how much the finance charges will add to the total cost of the car.**

D. **Calculate the impact of the monthly payments on your budget.**

E. **Calculate how the total cost and the monthly payments would vary if you made a larger down payment.**

F. **Write down your decision and reasons about a buying a car at this time.**

Your goal for the future should be to be totally debt free, especially for depreciating items such as cars. Buy a car within your budget. Drive it until it is totally paid for, and then save to buy the next one.

This Is Your Life

Applying what you learn to your present finances.

1. You should now have a record of your monthly expenses by category. Were you able to stay within the budgeted amounts for each category? If not, do you need to adjust the amount you have budgeted for each category—or simply work harder to stay within your budget?

2. Go on, that wasn't so bad. Why not fill out some new copies of the "Individual Account Sheets" (Form 3) for your personal budget categories? Then keep running records of your income and expenditures for the next month.

3. If you own your own car, are you making monthly payments? How much are you spending each month (including gas and maintenance) on transportation? Based on what you learned

in this lesson, are you getting the most for your money?

4. If you don't own a car, but use your parents' car, what do you contribute toward car expenses? Is this expense part of your budget?

5. Do you use public transportation? What percent of your NSI goes toward transportation? Weighing owning a car versus public transportation, which is most workable and affordable for you now?

FOR ADDITIONAL STUDY

Maintain your budget for a sixth and final month, recording another month's worth of income and expenses. Refer to the sixth month of examples in Appendix E.
To review how you are grasping the ideas of this lesson, take the following quiz.
1. True or False—It's better to lease a car, because you can give it back if necessary.
2. True or False—A new car depreciates faster than a used car.
3. True or False—New car financing is often at a lower rate than used car financing.
4. True or False—Leasing is less expensive than purchasing a new car.
5. True or False—Most low-cost loans for new cars are a means to sell the cars at higher prices or to sell higher-priced models.
6. The best source for a used car is usually:
   A. An auction.
   B. Used car lot.
   C. Parking lot.
   D. Personal contacts.
7. Usually the lowest cost loan is:
   A. "Add-on" interest.
   B. Collateral loan.
   C. Floor plan loan.
   D. At-risk loan.

BUYING A FIRST HOME

GETTING STARTED

Buying a home is not just a matter of choosing the house you like and moving in. Only a limited amount of your budget can go to housing and that amount must cover the mortgage payments, taxes, utilities, etc. Now that you understand how to budget your monthly income, you have a definite advantage over most young people.

Buying a home involves much more than just paying the mortgage. First, it is necessary to save enough money for your down payment (usually at least 10—20 percent of the sale price) and the fees and closing costs (another 2—5 percent). We'll take a look at mortgage loans, closing costs, insurance, and taxes.

STEP 1
Loan Sources for the First-Time Buyer

Where you borrow the money for your new home can make a big difference in what it costs to buy a home. The traditional sources are savings and loan (S & L) companies, banks, the government, and private lenders.

In this lesson, you will . . .
- Discover the loan sources available to first-time buyers;
- Learn the difference between an "adjustable rate mortgage" and a "fixed rate mortgage;"
- Compare the costs of thirty- and fifteen-year mortgages;
- Find out what closing costs one can expect when buying a house;
- Discover what insurance a home owner must purchase; Learn what items are usually included in the monthly mortgage payment.

When you borrow through a bank or savings and loan company, the interest rate is determined by the prevailing interest rate in the economy at that time.

However, there are usually several government programs available to aid first-time or low-income home buyers by providing loans at lower interest rates. The most widely known are:

Federal Housing Authority (FHA)—available to most average home buyers;

Veteran's Administration (VA)—available only to qualifying armed services veterans;

Housing and Urban Development (HUD)—usually only available in low-income urban areas.

Sometimes state or even local governments will allocate funds to aid first-time buyers.

STEP 2
Types of Mortgages

1. A Few Terms and Definitions

Mortgage This is a type of loan which gives the property to the lender if the borrower is unable to pay off the debt.

Collateral The property is the collateral (security or guarantee) for the loan.

Lien The contract states that the lender holds a lien (pronounced lean and meaning a legal right or bond) on the property.

Foreclose The lien holder can foreclose the mortgage (end the contract) and take possession of the property if the buyer cannot make the payments.

2. Fixed-Rate Mortgages

A fixed-rate mortgage is a simple-interest loan using the property as the collateral. The rates are fixed and cannot be raised, allowing the borrower to know exactly what the payments will always be. A fixed rate, thirty-year loan, will often be 2—4 percent higher than for an adjustable rate mortgage.

As inflation has increased in our economy, fewer home mortgage lenders are willing to lend money for long periods (fifteen to thirty years) at fixed interest rates.

Their reluctance is understandable if you look at an example. Suppose a lender issued a thirty-year, fixed-rate mortgage at 10 percent, but in five years, because of inflation, the prevailing interest rates went up to 17 percent (as they did in 1981). The lender's earnings are fixed at 10 percent per year for the next twenty-five years, but payouts (the savings accounts of depositors) are at 17 percent. Fortunately for everyone, interest rates came down, but you can see right away that the mortgage lender would have had a real problem if the rates had stayed high.

3. Adjustable-Rate Mortgages (ARM)

To overcome their problem with fixed rate mortgages, lenders have created adjustable-rate mortgages (ARMs). An ARM allows the homeowner's interest rate to be adjusted annually according to a predetermined index (usually the prime lending rate).

To protect the borrower, most ARMs have a maximum rate of increase each year and a limit on the total maximum rate that can be charged. Usually the limits are a 1 percent increase per year with a maximum rate of 4—6 percent above the initial rate.

The attractive aspect of ARMs to the borrower is that they are usually given at an initially lower rate than the available fixed-rate mortgages. However, there is no guarantee that they will remain lower—it's somewhat of a gamble.

Anyone considering an ARM would be well advised to budget for increases. A 1 percent increase in a $100,000 mortgage is approximately $63 per month. A 5 percent increase can raise the mortgage payments by over $317 per month!

4. Fifteen Versus Thirty-Year Mortgages

When purchasing a house, it is often tempting to get the most house for the smallest monthly payment. This usually means spreading the payments out over as long a period as possible—usually over thirty years. Sometimes, this is fine. However, it can be rather shocking to see how much more one must pay in interest by lengthening the mortgage.

Sometimes it is better to accept "less" house, if necessary, so you can get a shorter mortgage.

Take a look at these examples.

$100,000 FIXED-RATE MORTGAGE AT 10.5 PERCENT

	30 Years	15 years	Difference
Monthly Payment	$ 914.74	$ 1,105.40	$ 190.66
Total Interest	$229,306.40	$ 98,972.00	$130,334.40
Ultimate Cost	$329,306.40	$198,972.00	$130,334.40

$75,000 FIXED-RATE MORTGAGE AT 10.5 PERCENT

	30 Years	15 years	Difference
Monthly Payment	$ 689.05	$ 829.05	$ 140.00
Total Interest	$171,978.00	$ 74,229.00	$ 97,749.00
Ultimate Cost	$271,978.00	$174,229.00	$ 97,749.00

$50,000 FIXED-RATE MORTGAGE AT 10.5 PERCENT

	30 Years	15 years	Difference
Monthly Payment	$ 457.37	$ 552.70	$ 95.33
Total Interest	$114,653.20	$ 49,486.00	$ 65,167.20
Ultimate Cost	$214,653.20	$149,486.00	$ 65,167.20

As you can see, a relatively small increase in monthly payments (about 20 percent) saves an enormous amount. Besides the savings of a shorter mortgage, lenders will often offer a fifteen-year, fixed-rate mortgages at 1—1.5 percent below those offered for a thirty-year mortgage. This is because the lender takes less risk of prevailing interest rates rising above a profitable level.

The only time a shorter mortgage would not be advantageous would be if you had a thirty-year mortgage at a very low interest rate and could be disciplined enough to invest that $100—$200 per month. But that's a rare arrangement and a difficult discipline.

STEP 3
Closing Costs

Besides needing the money for a down payment on a home, you also need cash to pay the other costs at time of closing or completing the purchase. That is why these costs are called "closing costs." Listed below are a few of the normal costs you can expect at closing before you can take possession of your new home.

1. Attorney fees. An attorney should be engaged to represent you at the closing and verify that all documents are correct. Usually the seller pays the cost of preparing the land deeds, notes, etc., but your cost for an attorney would normally be $150—$250. Get a clear agreement on these costs before hiring an attorney.

2. Recording costs. Your mortgage note and land deeds must be recorded at the county courthouse where the home is located. The recording fees will normally cost $50—$100.

3. Escrow accounts. Escrow means to place money in the care of a third party for a specific purpose. In a home escrow, the buyer is required to prepay expenses such as insurance and real estate taxes. Usually at least six months' prepaid taxes and insurance are required to be escrowed at closing. Together these can cost $500—$1,000.

The seller should also escrow funds for past taxes.

4. Loan fee points. "Points," as they are called, are closing costs charged by the lender. A point is 1 percent of the loan amount, and they come in two forms: discount points and loan fee points (or origination fees). Loan fee points are charged by the lender to cover the cost of processing the loan. (A separate loan application fee of $100—$300 may also be charged.)

5. *Discount points.* When loans are offered at low interest rates, the lenders usually charge an up-front fee to get a higher effective interest rate on your loan. These fees are commonly called "discount points."

Often, points and interest rates are "exchangeable" (within a range). You can get a lower interest rate if you are willing to pay more points. If you don't want to pay so many points, you have to take the higher rate. What you select should be based on the cash you have available and the amount you can afford in monthly payments.

Occasionally it is possible to get the seller to pay some of the points. This requires the seller to lower the selling price by that amount.

Many young adults have been shocked to find out when they went to sign the contracts on their new homes that they owed thousands of dollars in "points." If cash is not available, the points must be covered by taking out a larger mortgage. For instance, if you borrow $60,000 and pay three discount points, or $1,800, this is really borrowing only $58,200 that can be applied to the purchase of the home. However, you are paying interest on $60,000.

You can easily owe from $2,000–$5,000 at closing beyond your down payment on the home.

STEP 4
Home Insurance

There are three basic types of insurance that a typical homeowner is faced with selecting: property damage, mortgage insurance, and title insurance.

1. *Property damage insurance.* All mortgage lenders require that you carry insurance to protect the property which has been mortgaged. This will pay to repair or replace any physical damage from such things as a fire, flood, earthquake, or storm.

Additionally, you may elect to cover your furnishings, personal injury, liability, and relocation expenses if your home is damaged. When purchased all together, this insurance is called a "homeowner's policy." This type of insurance is available through most large insurance companies.

2. *Mortgage insurance.* This insurance will pay off the remaining mortgage if the insured dies. It is a type of declining life insurance (it declines as the mortgage balance declines). A good term insurance policy (see Lesson 7) is less costly than a typical mortgage insurance policy.

3. Title insurance. When you purchase real property (such as a home), an attorney hired by the seller does a title search of all the previous owners of the property. This search discovers if there are any outstanding claims against it. The attorney then prepares an "abstract," which is a summarized version of all the transactions on the property for as far back as records exist.

Title insurance will pay to defend in court your right of ownership to the property and will reimburse any loss you might have if you lose in court. Many mortgage lenders will require a buyer to purchase title insurance to protect their rights as well.

STEP 5
Total "Mortgage" Payments

When estimating what you can pay for a house, there are at least three things you must include that will usually be paid in your monthly mortgage payment.

1. P & I (Principal and Interest). The largest portion of your monthly payment will go to pay the principal (the actual money you borrowed) and interest (the fee the lender charges for loaning the money) of your mortgage. In the early years of a mortgage, the great majority of the payment will be applied to the interest.

2. Insurance. Most commonly, the mortgage company will escrow a portion of your monthly payment to cover your annual insurance premiums. A copy of your annual insurance bill goes to the mortgage company and is paid out of your escrowed funds.

3. Property taxes. Similarly, taxes are usually escrowed by the mortgage company and paid annually. You should discover what the past years' taxes have been. Be sure that money is escrowed by the seller for whatever portion of the unbilled year he or she has owned the home. (You don't want to be paying taxes for the time the seller owned the property.)

Taxes often add $50–$200 per month to the total mortgage payment. If you were buying a home on which you took out a $100,000 mortgage for fifteen years at 10.5 percent interest, your monthly payment could easily look like this:

P & I	$1,105
Insurance	50
Taxes	150
TOTAL	$1,305

NOTE: First-time homebuyers often find buying a condominium to be an excellent way to enter the housing market. Condos, in which some of the property is jointly owned by all the owners in the complex, often cost less than single family homes. However, the owner's association assesses fees (for maintenance and insurance of the "common" areas) which must be calculated into the monthly cost.

A. **Now, using Form 10, "What Home Can You Buy?" go through the exercise of determining what price you can afford for a home.**

B. **Then try to locate three possible homes (and/or condominiums) in that price range in the real estate section of a local newspaper.**

This Is Your Life

Applying what you learn to your present finances.

1. Hang in there with recording each expenditure under its proper category. Remember to deduct the amount spent from the amount budgeted to give you a running total of what you have left to spend in that category.

2. When or under what conditions do you think young people should begin contributing toward housing if they live in their parents' home?

3. What do your parents think about this?

4. What would be a fair amount in your case?

5. Discover what your costs will be to rent an apartment or house in your community. What are the typical "up-front" charges (i.e., first and last month's rent, security deposit, cleaning fee, etc.)?

FOR ADDITIONAL STUDY

1. Find one person (family) who has purchased a home within the last five years and who is willing to share with you the financial details of the purchase.

   What was the purchase price?

   What was their down payment?

   What were the closing costs apart from the down payment?

   What rate of interest do they pay?

   For how long is their mortgage?

   What are the total monthly payments (P & I, insurance, taxes)?

   Are there any aspects of the deal they wish they would have done differently?

2. To review how you are grasping this lesson, take the following quiz.

   1. True or False—The seller usually pays the "closing costs."
   2. True or False—The buyer usually prepays a portion of the real estate taxes.
   3. True or False—Title insurance protects against any potential damage to the property.
   4. True or False—Mortgage insurance is required by most lenders.
   5. Reduced interest rates for mortgage loans usually require:
      A. Higher monthly payments.
      B. Discount points.
      C. Service fees.
      D. Prepaid monthly interest.
   6. An example of a subsidized government lending agency is:
      A. HEP.
      B. BMW.
      C. FHA.
      D. FFA.
   7. True or False—A thirty-year mortgage usually has a higher interest rate than a fifteen-year mortgage.
   8. The discount points on a mortgage:
      A. Are charged by the lender.
      B. Reduce the payments.
      C. Can be used for free food.
      D. None of the above.
   9. Most lenders require which insurance?
      A. Health insurance.
      B. Collision insurance.
      C. Property insurance.
      D. Life insurance.

LOOKING FOR WORK

GETTING STARTED

The best budget in the world won't work without the necessary income. However, we have saved the subject of finding a good job until the last because it is seldom the first thing that needs improvement in order to have all the money you need. Wise management of what you have must come first. Too often the average person's first response to money problems is: "If I only had a little more income." As important as a good job is, though, more income is seldom the answer.

Now that you have learned how to manage what you have, you are ready to talk about looking for work.

Many high school students want part-time jobs. Often, these part-time jobs help finance higher education and can become stepping stones which lead to lifetime careers. For this reason, high school part-time jobs are to be taken as seriously as an adult's profession.

In this lesson, you will . . .
- **Better understand where to look for jobs (full-time or part-time) and how to apply for them;**
- **Learn how to use employment agencies;**
- **Develop your confidence in what you can offer a potential employer;**
- **Learn how to answer want ads.**

Before you can get a good job or receive training for a profession, you must know how to go about it. One should go into the job market with a good attitude about why and how to work.

With some wise preparation and help from those around you, you need never be trapped in a fruitless job as so many are today. It all begins with a first step, and this lesson will help you get started on the right foot.

Looking for work means just that: looking. A person who is seeking employment needs to know the various ways and places to look.

1. Referral by someone to a particular job has special advantages. You may hear about a position before it is otherwise widely advertised. If your acquaintance is

respected, you can benefit by his or her recommendation. Always pursue such an option, as it is often the most effective way to land a job.

2. Pursuing help wanted ads in your local newspaper is always possible even when personal connections fail.

3. Going through a state or private employment agency opens other options.

4. Going from business to business and asking to apply for work is less likely to turn up a job, but it should not be overlooked.

In this lesson we are going to concentrate on the second and third options.

STEP 1
Pursuing Help Wanted Ads

Look for Help Wanted ads in weekly and daily newspapers in the section called "Help Wanted." Large city newspapers often list job categories such as "professional," "business," and "general." Usually, Sunday papers carry the most ads.

The manner in which you answer an ad establishes the first impression a potential employer has of you. Want ads usually give you the basic information needed to apply for a job. Sometimes the wage offered is given. Often a phone number is printed. This is so the employer can screen applicants by telephone and save both the employer and potential employee time.

Some ads detail the training necessary for jobs, and most require at least a high school education. However, for part-time jobs, this is usually not the case, and many employers of part-time workers are even willing to hire high-school students.

It's important to read the want ads thoroughly and reply exactly as the ad says. An employer often gets his or her initial impression by the way an applicant answers the ad. A person who can't follow directions given in the ad probably won't follow directions on the job.

A. **Read through the examples of help wanted ads on the next page:**

HELP WANTED ADS

1. FULL-TIME OPENINGS. A few positions available for full-time tellers. Join the friendly staff of a large, busy bank. Opportunity for future growth. Excellent benefits package. Apply at the personnel office of the FIVE-CENTS SAVINGS BANK, second floor, 206 Essex St. An excellent training program will be starting on Monday morning.

2. RESPONSIBLE PERSON wanted to deliver parts, afternoons. Must be experienced driver with a good driving record. Three days a week. Call 948-2495, ask for Joe for an interview.

3. PAINTER. Paint spraying experience required. Apply: MODERN PLATING CO., 2340 Washington St., 445-4400.

4. ASST. MANAGER. Summer help needed. 44 hrs./wk., sm. athletic store. Salary commensurate with exp. Call Ann, 531-2480.

5. TV REPRESENTATIVE. Immed. opening for person to rent portable televisions at a local maternity hospital; weekends only. Call 782-8402. 9 am till noon.

6. AUTO AND HARDWARE. Salesperson. Commission only. Good benefits. 356-4303.

7. CLASS II DRIVER wanted immediately. Call 768-6909.

8. TEMPORARY POSITIONS, all types. 24 years of placement experience to work for you. Call AID INC. 744-1326.

9. TAXI DRIVERS to drive late model, well maintained cars. FM Radio, lease systems, keep balance, 2-way radios. We will help you obtain a taxi license. 269-9483.

10. DELIVERY SERVICE. Drivers with own vehicle wanted for courier service. A chance to earn money while driving your own vehicle. Call Mr. Ed., 787-2022.

11. PART-TIME employment. General house cleaning. Car necessary. Call Carolyn, 531-9029.

12. ASTHMATICS to participate in a 5-day pharmaceutical research project. Must be in good health otherwise. Call 522-0303.

NOTE: Many of the preceding help wanted ads do not mention work experience, but others do have some requirements.

B. Answer the following questions about the ads:
1. Which job or jobs would be suitable for a full-time student?
2. Why would ad number 9 not be suitable for a student?
3. What do you think "commission only" in ad number 6 means?

STEP 2
Using Employment Agencies

Sometimes jobs offered in the want ads are placed by an employment agency. Private employment agencies work in two ways. When they list a position and say, "fee paid," this means that the employer will pay all the associated fees.

However, if "fee paid" is not mentioned in the want ad, it is likely that the applicant will have to pay the agency for finding him or her a job. This fee usually is a certain percentage of the employee's first month's pay. The fee varies from agency to agency.

Sometimes when you can't find employment on your own, an

agency is the best way to seek help. However, you need to be sure you have exhausted all your own resources before paying an agency to find you a job.

Answer the following three questions:
1. Which job in the previous ads would be through an agency?
2. Who would most likely pay the expenses of the agency?
3. When is it best to use an agency? Why?

NOTE: State employment agencies don't charge fees. Though people more often use them when looking for full-time work, they can be a good resource for part-time work as well.

STEP 3
Developing Your Confidence

Often teens feel insecure about having the necessary experience to get started in a job market. "How can I get experience if I don't have the job?" is a common question.

However, there may be experiences in your background which would qualify you for a job.

A. Answer the following questions to identify some of the experience you have which may help qualify you for a job:
   1. What skills has your life at home taught you which might be helpful in serving others?
      a. Do you have younger brothers or sisters in your home? This could have prepared you to do child care.
      b. What about lawn mowing, hedge clipping, being a farmer's helper, wood cutting and splitting, snow removal, house cleaning (spring or fall), or perhaps painting or papering?
   2. What academic skills have you developed?
      a. Are you especially good in math, English, or other subjects? If you are, perhaps you might be a good tutor to a lower-grade student.
      b. What skills have you learned in school—have you taken typing, filing, shorthand, shop classes, automotive mechanics, sewing, or cooking? These are all marketable skills.
   3. What skills and personal qualities have you developed in outside of school activities such as athletics or clubs?
B. Think about your personal skills, and come up with a potential part-time job you could do which would use some of those skills.

C. **Review the ads below. Then, on a separate sheet of paper, write a brief ad of your own, using twenty words or less.**

AT YOUR SERVICE

1. WILL DO ODD JOBS, assist elderly and disabled, house cleaning, walk dogs, run errands, shovel walks, and baby-sitting. Call Kellie 623-3008.

2. QUALITY PAINTING and light carpentry with reasonable rates. Call 632-9385.

3. LOVE AND CARE given to young child. Two and up. Learn and play. Call Judy 622-7898.

4. WANTED steady work. Also will do light trucking and odd jobs. Ask for Elaine 623-1077

5. HOUSE CLEANING for the busy professional or to prepare for holidays. $5/hour. 623-3034.

6. PET CARE. Dependable teen to care for your pet at home while you travel. Have transportation. 632-1901

7. CATERING. Will help with your party. Good cook, server. $7.00/hour. Cathy 634-0094

STEP 4
Answering an Ad

Once you have decided to answer a want ad placed by an employer, you should read the ad carefully and do exactly as the ad instructs. The way you answer the ad will be the first impression you will make on a potential employer.

Want ads are usually written in the shortest manner possible, with just enough information to give the reader instructions for making contact.

Answering by telephone. When answering an ad that requires you to telephone, you should follow good phone etiquette when you make your call.

You probably use the phone daily, but do you know there are good manners involved in speaking on the phone?

This first contact is very important. Effective use of the phone is a means of communication that requires thought and planning when answering an ad. A phone call is not like a letter which can be re-read. This first contact must be clear and concise. A misunderstanding could eliminate you as a prospective employee.

Some good rules to follow are:
1. **Read the ad carefully.** If a specific person is to be contacted, ask for that person. If that person is not available, ask when he or she will be in and promptly call at the specified hour.

2. **Speak clearly,** loudly enough, and slowly enough so that you can be understood easily.

3. **Identify yourself as soon as the person answers.** Say something like this (with the appropriate names, etc.): "Hello, this is Bill Kramer. I'm calling about your ad in today's Tribune for a part-time sales clerk in your shoe department."

4. **Be ready to talk.** Have ready any information you think an employer might ask. Write out anything you think he or she might ask on a note pad and have it by the phone. If you are very nervous, write down your name and age and other pertinent information such as the school you are attending and even the town that you live in. Don't take the chance of "drawing a blank" and causing yourself an embarrassing moment.

5. **Be a good listener.** Have paper and pencil ready to write down any specific instructions given to you. As in answering the ad initially, following instructions exactly will make a good impression. If you don't understand something or are unclear about anything, ask questions.

6. **Don't use this phone call to ask questions about salary or working conditions.** The phone call is simply a first step toward making an application for a job.

7. **Above all else, be pleasant, courteous and considerate.**

Responding by mail. Many ads will say, "Write for information..." and give an address. Don't call the newspaper in an attempt to get the name of the company or person who placed the ad. Most papers won't give out that information. Even if you do find out who placed the ad, still follow the instructions printed with the ad. **Here are six helpful tips:**

1. **Use a business letter format** that includes the date and your return address at the top of the page. If possible, your greeting should name your potential employer.

2. **Begin with a simple statement** such as, "I am applying for the job you advertised in today's Tribune." If you have been referred by someone else, say so. State the reasons that you want to work for this firm. Be brief and not flowery. If you have specific abilities or talents which apply to working for this employer, state them here.

3. **If the advertisement asks for your qualifications, list the information carefully.** Be honest and accurate and don't ever mislead by generalizations or exaggerations about your qualifications. List your education, your

experience (if you have any), your age and your complete address and phone number. If you have a resumé, include it. (See the next lesson for how to create a resumé.)

4. **End the letter with a short paragraph,** such as "I will be glad to meet for an interview at your convenience." Close with "Sincerely yours," and be sure you type your name under your signature.

5. **Use white, 8½″ x 11″, good, bond typing paper** (not the thin stuff). Be precise and as businesslike as you can. Never try to be artistic or unusual in an attempt to catch interest. Leave your pretty or cute stationery for a note to a friend.

6. **If it is possible, type your letter.** If a typewriter is not available to you, a handwritten letter is acceptable. However, write clearly and distinctly.

Applying in person. Some ads will give the company's name and tell you to go to their location. If you answer an ad like this, remember to be conscientious about your appearance and mannerisms. Your first impression could make or break your chance of getting beyond an application to an interview, and possibly a job.

Ultimately, every potential job requires a personal interview. The decision to hire or not to hire is greatly dependent on how you present yourself during this interview. The interview can be enhanced if you know the basic rules and are prepared to sell yourself to a prospective employer. **Follow these guidelines:**

1. **Dress to fit the job.** For instance, if you're applying for a position as a salesperson, it is appropriate for men to wear slacks with a coat and tie. Women should wear a business dress. However, if you're applying for a position as a warehouse stock person, slacks and a nice sports shirt would be appropriate. It's better to overdress a little than to underdress. For instance, worn-out jeans and a T-shirt leave a bad first impression.

2. **Bring a concise resumé of your qualifications and experience.** Even if you don't have a formal resumé, be sure to take a list of your past jobs. Include addresses, the name and phone number of your supervisor, and the accurate dates of your employment. Also, be sure you have your Social Security number with you. In the next lesson, we'll take a look at preparing a resumé. Then, in the lesson which follows, we'll work on preparing you for that face-to-face interview.

This Is Your Life

Applying what you learn to your present finances.

1. Based on two to three months of keeping track of your income and expenses, do you need to:
   • get a job?
   • work more hours in your present one?
   • change jobs?
   Why or why not?
2. If so, decide the following:
   a. What kind of job you want.
   b. How to locate such a job.
   c. How much per hour you need to make.
   d. How many hours you can work per week.

WRITING A SHARP RESUME

GETTING STARTED

The traditional and best way of communicating your background, abilities, and experience to a potential employer is through the "resumé," a written summary of the work-related assets you can bring to a job.

The resumé should outline your education, experience, interests, and activities. If you read an ad that says to send a resumé, you should be able to compile one with accuracy. The resumé is often the first tool employers use to screen unwanted applicants (similar to a phone call). So a well-planned and well-written resumé of your talents and abilities can be what gets you an interview and then a job.

In this lesson, you will . . .
- **Learn the basics of preparing a resumé;**
- **Discover the format for an effective resumé;**
- **Find out what not to include;**
- **Be guided through designing your own resumé;**
- **Learn the details of an effective cover letter for your resumé.**

STEP 1
Rules for Preparing Your Resume

A good resumé is usually one page in length (never more than two pages). It should outline your education, experience, interests, skills, and sometimes your job objectives.

It often gives the first impression of you and therefore, should be typed and done in a readable fashion. There are several ways to organize resumés, and no one is more right than another.

Always write and organize a resumé to fit the type of job that you are seeking. For example, if you're going after a job on a newspaper, be sure to include any honors you received when working on the high school newspaper. If you're preparing a resumé which will go to a variety of potential employers, you need to be able to look back at the most important things you have experienced and analyze those you feel would be most helpful in the job you are seeking.

Study these few basic rules about preparing a resumé:

1. **Your resumé should be brief.** Most people don't read them word for word, anyway. The longer you make it, the less of what's important may be read. You might think of a resumé as an advertisement for you.

2. **When typing your resumé, use columns, margins, capital letters and other devices to make your resumé** attractive and help the important parts to stand out. However, keep it business-like. Do not employ cute graphics or various sizes and styles of type (if you are using a computer).

3. **You may list your "Job Objectives."** This is optional to the first-time job seeker, especially a high school student who is willing to work at almost any job.

4. **Briefly list any courses which contribute to your ability to do the job.** Don't list all the courses you have taken. However, it is helpful to indicate briefly an area of emphasis if it contributes to your qualifications for the type of job you are seeking. Just be brief! If you took an academic course, but had some emphasis on business courses, say just that.

5. **Condense your listing of past jobs as briefly as possible.** Be completely honest, describing exactly what you did in each job.

6. **Emphasize the skills you have developed.** Your future employer is most interested in this and how it can apply to his or her company.

7. **Be ready to supply references** from other employers or anyone (not family) who can give a good reference about your working abilities and personal characteristics. You can either say, "References furnished upon request" or list at least three names, addresses, phone numbers, and job titles of people who will be references for you. The more prestigious a reference is, the better, provided the person truly knows you and will speak well of you.

NOTE: If you feel that you cannot adequately prepare your resumé, get help from schoolteachers, counselors and parents. Public libraries also have helpful books on this subject.

STEP 2
The Resumé Format

Study the following generally accepted format for preparing your resumé. Remember that accuracy, style, and neatness make a resumé readable and make a good impression.

Sample Resumé Format

1. NAME:
   Name
   Complete Address
   Complete Phone Number

2. EDUCATION:
   (If you have specific job objectives, they should precede this block under the heading of "JOB OBJECTIVES.")

   Include in your education block the name of the last school you attended. List the number of years you attended or the dates; the year you graduated; if college, the degree you received; and your major fields of study. When listing your schools, list the highest education first and descend to your high school education. Do not include any schools below that.

3. EXPERIENCE:
   This part of your resumé is your work history. You should list your jobs or positions you have held in reverse chronological order. Begin with your last job and descend down in order by years. For each job you should list the company's name and city and brief description of your position. If you attained specific achievements in this company, list these, such as awards, inventions, etc.

4. OTHER EXPERIENCE OR ACTIVITIES:
   This block should include school, civic, and personal activities or hobbies that might be of interest to an employer. Awards of specific nature should be included here. Offices held in church, civic or school organizations should be written here.

What Not to Include in a Resumé

1. The salary you desire. This should be discussed in an interview.
2. Your age, your marital status, and children.
3. Any handicaps you may have. If you are seeking a position which you honestly believe you can handle, despite a handicap, you need not mention a handicap.

Specifics of the Format

1. Type the resumé, and make it free of spelling or grammatical errors.
2. Leave space between sections of the resumé—especially areas you want to stand out. Remember, your resumé advertises you.
3. Try to limit the resumé to one page or two at the most.
4. Having your resumé professionally printed is desirable,

especially when you are applying for a full-time position. Never send a carbon or a poor quality photocopy.

STEP 3
Designing Your Resumé

A. **Gather the information needed to prepare your resumé.**
B. **Complete a copy of Form 11, "Creating Your Resumé."**
The following is an example of a typical resumé.

A Sample Resumé

```
Paul Harper
234 Riverview Rd.
Tarsus, GA 00089
123-456-7890

EDUCATION:      1982—present
                Georgia Technical Institute
                Atlanta, GA
                Business Administration/Computer Sciences

                1978—1982
                Centerville High School
                Tarsus, GA
                Academic courses with business administration

EXPERIENCE:     1982—present
                Technical Computer Time Sharers
                Atlanta, GA
                Part-time computer programmer

                1980—1982
                McDougall's Fast Foods
                Tarsus, GA
                Cashier/cook

                1979
                Available Summer Camp
                Gorcus, KY
                Summer counselor

                1978
                Midriff Realty
                Tarsus, GA
                Grounds work

ACTIVITIES:     Society of Future Computer Designs, Georgia Tech-
                nical Institute. Active member and vice-president.

                Editor, Computer Design News, Georgia Technical
                Institute. Organized each monthly issue. Duties in-
                cluded heading up reporters, organizing workloads,
                and editing the paper.

REFERENCES:     Available upon request.
```

STEP 4
Writing a Cover Letter

A cover letter should be placed on top of your resumé to communicate more personally with the potential employer. The letter can make sure you are considered for the specific job in which you are interested.

An employer may be considering applicants for more than one job. For the most part, resumés look alike. Because of this, applicants sometimes are not given careful consideration. The cover letter can be the element that catches the eye.

Your cover letter should draw attention to your resumé. It should be done in a businesslike form as described in the last lesson. It should be brief, and yet explain who you are and why you want to be considered for the job. It should not exceed one short page.

Write a cover letter similar to the sample below, addressing it to a specific company in your area:

---

234 Riverview Rd.
Tarsus, GA 00089
[Current Date]

Mr. Future Employer
2000 Business Dr.
Atlanta, GA 00056

Dear Mr. Employer:

I am writing to apply for employment with your firm. I have some basic computer skills which I hope could serve you well.

I appreciate your company's reputation for helping college students work their way through school. I have been accepted at Georgia Technical Institute, where I want to study computer science and business administration. I feel I could be a good employee for you while pursuing my studies.

I have attached a current resumé. It outlines my education, employment experience, and other activities that have enhanced my job skills in the area of computers. References are available upon request.

I hope to have an interview with you soon. I am available during the day until 4:00 p.m. and have my own transportation.

Thank you for your time and for considering my resumé and possible employment with your firm.

Sincerely yours,

Paul Harper

Encl.

This Is Your Life

Applying what you learn to your present finances.

1. Continue recording your actual expenses in your appropriate budget categories.
2. If you are seriously looking for a (new) job, send copies of the resumé you prepared for this lesson to actual places where you would like to apply. Try to discover the name of the personnel manager in charge of hiring, and address your cover letter to him or her.

THE WINNING JOB INTERVIEW

GETTING STARTED

T he job interview is the final and most important step in being hired for a job.

If your application has been reviewed, your resumé and contents of your cover letter read, and you are asked to come in for an interview, then you are a serious candidate for the job. Remember that usually several others are also trying for this job.

Merely because you are selected for a job interview does not guarantee you a job. Sometimes the interview will convince both you and the employer that this is not the job for you.

If you do not get the first job you apply for, don't become discouraged. You can learn from each experience, even the negative ones. It is not unusual for a company to interview twenty people for a single job. Even though you may feel the job is perfect for you, the interviewer may not, or he or she may fail to recognize your abilities.

In this lesson, you will . . .
- **Learn what to do to prepare for a job interview;**
- **Discover how to behave and what to talk about during a job interview;**
- **Find out what kind of follow-up to your interview is appropriate.**

Remember that a good initial impression is important, but it doesn't automatically guarantee you the job. However, a bad initial impression will practically guarantee that you will not get the job.

The interview may be the potential employer's first look at you. Everything about you is important during this time. You need to be concerned about your personal physical appearance, but even more, your attitude will announce whether you are prepared to work willingly under this employer's leadership. Remember why you are at the interview: to show that you can do a specific job for the employer.

STEP 1
So, You've Got the Interview

When you have been called for a job interview, there are several things you should know before you arrive at the interview. You should prepare for the interview just as you would if you were actually going to work.

The person who is interviewing you knows exactly what the job will need and is considering whether you will fit the job. A job interview is the time when a potential employer sits down with you to ask specific questions which will help him or her choose a new employee. **Study these basic rules for making your first impression a good one:**

1. Be prepared. You need to be able to answer all questions about yourself, your background, and even your family life. Be specific and brief when answering questions. Don't, under any circumstances, exaggerate about your background. Have an extra copy of your resumé with you in case it has been misplaced.

2. Do some homework. If it is possible, learn a little about the company before your interview. What is the business? How is this business transacted? Be prepared by learning as much about the potential employer as possible. This will show your interest in the company's well-being.

3. Watch your appearance. Good grooming is a must. Most employers are impressed with a conservative and clean-cut look. Don't dress too casually or try to be "sexy." Forget blue jeans, fad shirts, and heavy makeup. Dark colors are the most conservative, and greens, browns and rust colors are good for women. Shine your shoes and spit out the gum. If you aren't familiar with proper dress for a particular job you are going after, seek out help in this area before going to the interview.

4. Be on time. Never keep an interviewer waiting for you. If there is any possibility of a transportation delay (traffic jam, late bus, etc.), leave early enough to compensate. If you get to your destination fifteen to thirty minutes early, that's much better than arriving breathlessly at the last moment or being late. You can wait in your car or walk around the block during the extra time and get to the company's door about ten minutes ahead of time.

STEP 2
During the Interview

As you consider these six tips, think of why each one is important.

1. Relax. Wait for the interviewer to tell you where to sit. Look at the interviewer and make eye contact when he or she is talking and you are answering. The first few minutes of an interview should be spent in getting acquainted.

2. Listen. Be careful to listen to the name of the one interviewing you, if you don't know it beforehand. The sweetest sound to anyone's ear is the sound of his or her own name. Listen precisely to questions or comments made by the interviewer. Don't add small talk or chitchat. Don't tell funny jokes.

3. Think before you speak. Then answer all questions honestly and completely. Avoid cryptic yes-and-no answers to questions that can be answered more fully.

4. Let the interviewer introduce salary. Don't try to discuss money until the interviewer brings it up. The interviewer knows that it's important to you and will discuss it with you if you are being seriously considered. (The only time you should bring it up is if you are offered the job without money being mentioned. Obviously, you shouldn't say yes until there is a clear commitment on your wages.)

5. Watch what you say and do.
- Don't use slang or make uncomplimentary comments about former employers or co-workers. Any old resentments you express will cause the interviewer to suspect that you will develop the same attitudes toward him or her.
- Don't shake hands unless the interviewer prompts it.
- Don't accept an interviewer's offer of refreshments unless he or she takes refreshments, too, and urges your participation.
- Don't collapse into the chair or put your feet on any furniture.
- Don't comb your hair, file your nails, etc., during an interview.

6. Ask questions. If you have questions, feel free to ask them. Don't walk away from an interview and "wish" you had asked.

7. Be gracious as you leave. Many potential jobs are lost as the interviewee walks out the door. This can easily happen if you let down your guard or don't display good manners during the last minutes of an interview. Sometimes this is the result of becoming too comfortable or familiar. Also, if you are not offered the job on the spot, it is tempting to become disappointed. Make sure you do not express a sour or flippant attitude that will turn off an employer. Keep your attitude positive; remain polite and expectant. Don't beg, plead or cry to get the job.

STEP 3
The Follow-Up
Plan what you will do after the interview.

1. Wait. A job offer will seldom be made during an interview. Usually several people are being interviewed, and the employer wants to select the best person for the job. Therefore, you cannot expect a direct answer to whether you've gotten the job at the interview. Your answer will probably come through a phone call or letter within one to two weeks after the interview. If you have not heard by this time (or the time designated by the interviewer), it is appropriate for you to call and check on the process.

2. Send a thank-you note to the person who interviewed you. This is gracious and is unlikely to appear too anxious. Thank your interviewer for the time and consideration that he or she gave you. It will make a good impression, and it will keep you on the mind of your potential employer.

3. Keep looking and applying. Like everything else in life, you will get better at job interviews only through practice—as long as you practice the right things. Don't let a turn down (or even a series of turn downs) keep you from pursuing your goal of finding the job that is right for you.

4. Once you get a job, how well you do is dependent on additional skills. These include timeliness, self-discipline, courteousness, training, etc. Remember that what you do on the job and how you do it will speak more clearly than anything you have said about yourself in your application, resume, or interview.

STEP 4
Wrap Up

Congratulations! You've completed a course that will improve your ability to manage your money and land a job that can provide for your needs.

To test the skills you have learned, take the following review quiz. If you have problems with any of the questions, go back and review.

Match the Following:

1. Total income before deductions

2. Available funds after taxes

3. The portion belonging to the IRS

4. Account sheets are used for

5. When you borrow money

A. Income tax
B. File
C. Gross
D. Loss
E. Inflation
F. Loan
G. Budget control
H. Sales tax
I. Net spendable
J. Liability

Identify True or False

6. True or False—Income taxes are mandatory.
7. True or False—Unscheduled expenses cannot be budgeted.
8. True or False—Add-on interest is the cheapest.
9. True or False—Adjustable rate mortgages are illegal.
10. True or False—Health insurance is optional.
11. True or False—Your resume should include your age.

Select the Correct Answer:

12. A banking service that keeps your checks from ''bouncing'' when you have insufficient funds to cover them is called:
    A. Automatic teller.
    B. Master Charge.
    C. Overdraft protection.
    D. None of the above.
13. Life insurance purchased for a specified time is called:
    A. Whole-life.
    B. Gross rate.
    C. Declining.
    D. Term.

14. A contract to take out a loan to buy a house is called:
    A. An abstract.
    B. Mortgage.
    C. Lien.
    D. Deficiency agreement.
15. How many categories are there in this course's budget system?
    A. Five.
    B. Ten.
    C. Twelve.
    D. One.

This Is Your Life

Applying what you learn to your present finances.

Evaluate the records you have kept of your actual income and expenses for the past three months:

1. What changes, if any, have projecting a budget and keeping records of actual expenses made on your spending patterns?
2. What changes would you like to make?
3. What needs to happen to make those changes possible?

GIVING TO GOD

GETTING STARTED

In many ways, giving is a Christian's spiritual barometer. In other words, it measures where you are spiritually.

Just as a barometer doesn't cause the weather, neither does the presence or absence of giving make someone more or less spiritual. However, if you understand how to read a barometer properly, you can tell a great deal about the weather. In the same way, when you understand giving, you can gain some very important insight into your spiritual health by looking at your giving patterns.

In this lesson, you will . . .
- **Learn why Christians should give to God's work;**
- **Find out how we can give to God;**
- **Discover the four levels of giving in which Christians are encouraged to participate;**
- **Consider your level of giving to the Lord.**

STEP 1
Why Should the Christian Give?

Consider the following reasons why Christians should give to God:

Do we give to the church because God needs our money? In practical terms, our local church does need the support of every participant in order to continue its particular programs. Yet, God actually owns everything and doesn't need anything from us. In Psalm 50:10-12, God reminds us,

"For every beast of the forest is Mine,
The cattle on a thousand hills.
I know every bird of the mountains,
And everything that moves in the field is Mine.
If I were hungry, I would not tell you;
For the world is Mine, and all it contains."

(All Scriptures used in this lesson are from The Holy Bible, New International Version, © 1973, 1978, 1984 by the International Bible Society. Used by permission of Zondervan Bible Publishers.)

Therefore, why do we give to God?

The basic reason we give to God is for our own well-being. Giving reminds us that He is the owner of all that we have, and we have been entrusted to manage on His behalf. When we try keeping money or possessions all to ourselves, we reveal a serious problem in our view of life.

When we claim ownership of money and possessions, we inevitably look at every other aspect of our life the same way. We want to be in charge. We begin to think of God as our servant, duty-bound to help us when we call upon Him.

Rather, we should see ourselves as God's servants, ready always to do His will. That is what it means to call Him, "Lord." Lord means ruler, owner, sovereign, king.

Giving to God is so important because it reminds us who He is, who we are, and what our relationship should be to the things He has allowed us to manage in His name.

STEP 2
How Do We Give to God?

So, you may wonder, if God owns everything and therefore doesn't personally need anything, how can I give anything of significance to Him?

The answer can be found in the way God has set up the world. While it is possible for God to shower manna from heaven to feed the hungry, that is not His usual method of meeting people's needs. Usually, when someone is needy and unable to provide, God touches the heart of another person to share.

Look up the following Scriptures and match them to the actions on the right. You will discover several ways that we can give to God by meeting others' needs.

1. Malachi 3:10a	A. Support for ministers.
2. 1 Timothy 5:17,18	B. Helping needy relatives.
3. 2 Corinthians 8:13-15	C. Supporting missionaries.
4. 1 Timothy 5:8	D. Funding church programs.
5. Matthew 25:37-40	E. Sharing with Christians.
6. Luke 10:1-7	F. Giving to the poor.

Each of these kinds of giving pleases God. As Jesus said in one of the passages above, "To the extent that you did it . . ., you did it to Me." So, giving as God wants us to give is counted as giving to Him.

STEP 3
Four Levels of Giving

The ways we give can be understood on four different levels: the tithe, giving out of obedience, giving out of our abundance, and sacrificial giving. **Examine these four levels of giving to discover what each one involves:**

1. Giving the Tithe.

The word "tithe" literally means a tenth. It is the least amount God ever asked His people to give.

The first time we see any mention of a tithe in the Bible is in Genesis 14:20. Abraham was returning home from a great battle when he was met by Melchizedek. (Many Bible scholars believe that Melchizedek was actually Jesus Christ, Himself.) Abraham certainly recognized that Melchizedek represented the most high God. Consequently, Abraham gave him a tithe, or tenth.

Picture Abraham, a mighty leader whose army had defeated a powerful enemy. Why would he, with all his warriors by his side, give away a tenth of all that he had to a priest? The reason was that Abraham was acknowledged that God was much greater than he was. He admitted God's ownership of all that he had. That was the purpose of Abraham's tithe, and it remains the same today.

In Malachi 3:10, God's Word says,

> "Bring the whole tithe into the storehouse, that there may be food in my house. Test me in this," says the Lord Almighty, "and see if I will not throw open the floodgates of heaven and pour out so much blessing that you will not have room enough for it."

Here we find God not only instructing us to give the tithe, but He also promises to bless those who tithe freely.

A. **Turn to Malachi 3:6-12 to find why God gave the people this reminder.**

B. **Answer these three questions:**
   - What was happening in their lives?
   - What does the passage say would be the consequences of giving the whole tithe?
   - What would logically be the consequences of not doing so?

2. Giving Out of Obedience.

In Matthew 23:23, Jesus scolded the Pharisees. Even though they carefully tithed such minor things as the herbs from their garden, they "neglected the more important matters of the law—justice and mercy and faithfulness." Jesus affirmed their tithing, but He said that the Law called them to go further.

In verse 25, He said that they were "full of greed and self-indulgence." Obedience to God calls for something more than a legal observance of tithing, because it is possible to tithe to God and still be cruel to people in need.

Two chapters later, Jesus explained what God expects in the way of true justice and mercy:

> Then the King will say to those on His right, "Come, you who are blessed by My Father; take your inheritance, the kingdom prepared for you since the creation of the world. For I was hungry and you gave me something to eat, I was thirsty and you gave me something to drink, I was a stranger and you invited me in; I needed clothes and you clothed me, I was sick, and you looked after me; I was in prison and you came to visit me" (Matt. 25:34-36).

A. According to this passage, how had this giving to Jesus been accomplished?

B. What would be an obedient response when you encounter someone in need?

C. What does this say to you about the kinds of giving you should be doing?

3. Giving Out of Our Abundance.

Sometimes we may be saving for a legitimate future need such as education, retirement, a home, etc. But along the way we encounter someone or some worthy project where the need is greater. At that point, when we choose to give out of our savings, we are giving out of our abundance. This is usually very difficult because it means giving up something we truly desire.

That is why Jesus warned us so often about the dangers of "riches" as in Luke 12:15-21.

> Then He said to them, "Watch out! Be on your guard against all kinds of greed; a man's life does not consist in the abundance of his possessions." And He told them this parable: "The ground of a certain rich man produced a good crop. He thought to himself, 'What shall I do? I have no place to store my crops.' Then he said, 'This is what I'll do. I will tear down my barns and build bigger ones, and there I will store all my grain and my goods. And I'll say to myself, "You have plenty of good things laid up for many years. Take life easy; eat, drink and be merry."' But God said to him, 'You fool! This

very night your life will be demanded from you. Then who will get what you have prepared for yourself?' This is how it will be with anyone who stores up things for himself, but is not rich toward God."

A. What is this story teaching about saving for the future?
B. Why are riches so dangerous?

4. Sacrificial Giving.

Sacrificial giving means giving up a "need" to help someone who may have even greater needs. John the Baptist described this attitude in Luke 3:11. "The man with two tunics should share with him who has none, and the one who has food should do the same."

Jesus illustrated the same approach to giving in Luke 21:1-4:

As he looked up, Jesus saw the rich putting their gifts into the temple treasury. He also saw a poor widow put in two very small copper coins. "I tell you the truth," he said, "this poor widow has put in more than all the others. All these people gave their gifts out of their wealth; but she out of her poverty put in all she had to live on."

You might say, "But if I give up a need, won't I end up suffering want?"

That's a good question, and Jesus answered it directly. He said, "But seek first his kingdom and his righteousness, and all these things will be given to you as well" (Matt. 6:33). The "things" Jesus mentioned were the basics of life—the food and drink and clothing that we all need.

This does not mean that Christians will never be poor. Some of us will be poor. But there's a difference between being poor and suffering want. One can be technically poor and have all the money needed.

God stations His people as witnesses in every level of life—from poor to rich. One of our missions in life is to show that God's grace is sufficient no matter what our experience—even when it's hard. As Paul said, "But he said to me, 'My grace is sufficient for you, for my power is made perfect in weakness.' Therefore I will boast all the more gladly about my weaknesses, so that Christ's power may rest on me" (2 Corinthians 12:9).

God's promise does not suggest that we can be lazy and expect God to feed us. Paul set down the rule: "If a man will not work, he shall not eat" (2 Thessalonians 3:10). Laziness is not consistent with righteousness.

But God has promised to care for the righteous, to meet our basic needs. King David said, "I was young and now I am old, yet I have never seen the righteous forsaken or their children begging bread" (Ps. 37:25). Similarly, Solomon declared, "The Lord does not let the righteous go hungry" (Proverbs 10:3).

NOTE: There are obviously times of disaster, famine and war, in which *everyone* suffers. Christians are not exempt from the consequences of living in a world marred by sin. Repeatedly in Scripture we read of God's people enduring great hardships along with everyone else. We even read of suffering which came specifically because they were obeying God:

> "I have labored and toiled and have often gone without sleep; I have known hunger and thirst and have often gone without food; I have been cold and naked" (2 Corinthians 11:27).

Paul assured us that no hardship will ever take us out of God's loving presence:

> "Who shall separate us from the love of Christ? Shall trouble or hardship or persecution or famine or nakedness or danger or sword? . . . No, in all things we are more than conquerors through him who loved us" (Romans 8:35).

STEP 4
Making a Commitment

1. Take time to calculate your real, personal income (the amount you have used for "This is Your Life"). As carefully as you can, estimate all the money you have received over the last three months—include regular earnings, occasional odd-jobs, and any allowance you might receive.

2. Divide that total amount by three to get your average monthly income.

3. Then take time to consider prayerfully whether you can fill in and sign the following document as a prayer to God.

Dear Lord,
Thank you for caring for me in both small and big ways. Thank you for providing food, clothes, and housing for me.
Thank you for providing my average income of $_____ per month. I am hereby acknowledging that it all belongs to You. I understand that I am not the owner of this money, but I am Your steward in managing it and all the other things You have given to me.

In gratefulness to You for entrusting me with managing it and in recognition that it truly belongs to You, I want to commit myself to returning _____ percent to You on a regular basis for the next year.
This amounts to $_____ per month.
Signed: _____

Date: _____

This Is Your Life

Applying what you learn to your present finances.

1. While it's a drag remembering to write down what you spend, it's a crucial step in learning to manage your money now.

2. In this lesson you considered making a commitment to set aside a percentage of your money each month for God's work. If so, how will you handle this reduction of your NSI? How will you adjust the percentages or amounts you've allotted to other categories? Remember, all categories must still add up to 100 percent of your NSI, but charitable contributions (like taxes) are calculated from your gross (total) income.

FOR ADDITIONAL STUDY

1. Onto the end of your last month's budget records, incorporate the following variations:
   a. Your washing machine broke down—beyond repair. You must purchase a new one at a budget-busting $400.
   b. If you have been practicing charitable giving, you have just received a tax refund because of overpayment of your income taxes. (Be sure to use a "bank deposit" for recording your tax refund into your records.) The government allows you to deduct authorized charitable giving from your gross income before calculating your net taxable income. Figure out what your refund is this way:
      1. Multiply your monthly charitable giving by twelve (12).
      2. Subtract this amount from your gross annual income.
      3. Multiply Line 2 by your tax percentage rate. (See Appendix A.).
      4. Multiply your old monthly tax by twelve (See Form 1.).
      5. Subtract Line 3 from Line 4. This is the amount of your refund.
         Note: In real life it is not this simple nor would you receive this much of a refund. The reason is that your Social Security contribution is figured before deductions while only your other taxes can benefit from allowable deductions in calculating your net taxable income.)

2. To review how you are grasping the ideas of the tithe, take the following quiz.
   1. True or False—Tithing is one of the Ten Commandments.
   2. True or False—Abraham was the first tither.
   3. True or False—Tithing eliminates all financial problems.
   4. True or False—Giving out of obedience is only for church leaders.
   5. True or False—God may ask you to give money your family needs.
   6. The widow gave in what manner?
   7. The rich farmer's mistake was:
      A. He built too many barns.
      B. He stole his neighbor's sheep.
      C. He was greedy.
      D. He should have grown soybeans.

JOB DESCRIPTIONS

Job Description (Job 1):

Your job is: **A PILOT**

Salary: $30,000 per year ($2,500 per month)

Tax Rate: 30 percent of gross income (includes state, federal and FICA)

Example: $30,000 x 30% = $9,000/year

Cash down payments available:
  House = $8,000; Auto = $5,000

Paycheck:

HOP, SKIP & JUMP AIRLINES   No. XXXX
999 Out-in-the
Boondocks, ST 00000

Pay to the
Order of: _____ (Your name) _____ $ 875.00 _____

***********$875.00************

Explanation of twice-per-month paycheck:

Gross Income $1,250.00
Deductions:
  FICA 187.50
  Federal 137.50
  State 50.00
  TOTAL DEDUCTIONS 375.00

ADJUSTED GROSS INCOME $875.00

JOB DESCRIPTION (Job 2)

Your job is: **A COMPUTER PROGRAMMER**
Salary: $24,000 per year ($2,000 per month)
Tax Rate: 28 percent of gross income (includes state,
                     federal and FICA)
                     Example: $24,000 x 28% = $6,720/year

Cash down payments available:
    House = $7,000; Auto = $4,500

Paycheck:

MICRO SYSTEMS, INC.
111 Almost
State-of-the, Art 00000

No. XXXX

Pay to the
Order of: _____ (Your name) _____ $ 720.00

***********$720.00***********

Explanation of twice-per-month paycheck:

Gross Income $1,000.00
Deductions:
    FICA 150.00
    Federal 100.00
    State 30.00
    TOTAL DEDUCTIONS 280.00

ADJUSTED GROSS INCOME $720.00

BUDGET NEEDS

For each of the budget categories 1-12, select the items you will need each month. In some categories (such as Food and Savings) your amount will be determined by a percentage of your monthly NSI (net spendable income) rather than by a choice among options.

Other categories have a variety of options from which to select. Enter your choices and their corresponding amounts on Form 1, "Monthly Income and Expenses."

1. Charitable Contributions

This category is voluntary and therefore not allocated. While the average per capita giving is between 1 percent and 3 percent, many people give far more. Enter the amount you wish to give, or leave this category blank.

2. Tax

This category is preassigned with your job. See Appendix A, "Job Description," for the amount.

3. Housing

Before selecting your particular house or apartment, be sure you have established the percentage and amount you want to spend on housing. If you are not able to get the house you want for that price, you will have to decide to either lower your housing expectations or adjust your category allotments to bring more money into your housing category from some other one. Remember, the total of all categories cannot exceed 100 percent of your Net Spendable Income (NSI).

H-1, Apartment

Description: two bedrooms, one bath, air conditioning, 850 square feet, near bus routes.

Monthly Costs:

Rent	$275
Insurance	25
Taxes	—
Electricity	70
Gas	—
Water	—
Sanitation	—
Telephone	50
Maintenance	—
Other	—
TOTAL	$420

H-2, Apartment

Description: three bedrooms, two baths, air conditioning, cable TV, 1,100 square feet, first month free rent.

Monthly Costs:

Rent	$540
Insurance	25
Taxes	—
Electricity	100
Gas	—
Water	—
Sanitation	—
Telephone	50
Maintenance	—
Other	—
TOTAL	$715

H-3, Condominium

Description: three bedrooms, two-and-a-half baths, 1,400 square feet, air conditioning, fireplace.
Price: $78,000
Down payment: $6,000

Monthly Costs:

Mortgage	$620
Insurance	70
Taxes	50
Electricity	100
Gas	25
Water	25
Sanitation	15
Telephone	75
Maintenance	110*
Other	—
TOTAL	$1,090

*Homeowners' Association Fee

H-4, House

Description: Three bedrooms, one-and-a-half baths, 1,200 square feet, older home, good shape, two fireplaces, one-acre lot.
Price: $62,000
Down payment: $5,500

Monthly Costs:

Mortgage	$510
Insurance	50
Taxes	40
Electricity	75
Gas	25
Water	—
Sanitation	—
Telephone	50
Maintenance	50
Other	—
TOTAL	$800

H-5, Mobile Home

Description: three bedrooms, two baths, air conditioning, furnished, 1,300 square feet.
Price: $23,000
Down payment: $3,000

Monthly Costs:

Mortgage	$230
Insurance	40
Taxes	10
Electricity	100
Gas	20
Water	10
Sanitation	15
Telephone	50
Maintenance	25
Space Rental	150
TOTAL	$650

H-6, Rental House

Description: three bedrooms, two baths, air conditioning, pool privileges, garage.

Monthly Costs:

Rent	340
Insurance	25
Taxes	—
Electricity	100
Gas	—
Water	15
Sanitation	10
Telephone	50
Maintenance	—
Other	—
TOTAL	$540

H-7, Home

Description: three bedrooms, two baths, shaded lot, nice area, must sell.
Price: $43,000
Down payment: $4,000

Monthly Costs:

Mortgage	$450
Insurance	50
Taxes	25
Electricity	50
Gas	10
Water	—
Sanitation	—
Telephone	50
Maintenance	50
Other	—
TOTAL	$685

H-8, Apartment

Description: two bedrooms, two baths, air conditioning, pool and tennis privileges, one-year lease.

Monthly Costs:

Rent	$225
Insurance	25
Taxes	—
Electricity	100
Gas	—
Water	—
Sanitation	—
Telephone	50
Maintenance	—
Other	—
TOTAL	$400

H-9, Apartment

Description: two bedrooms, one-and-a-half baths, air conditioning, government housing project.

Monthly Costs:

Rent	$150
Insurance	10
Taxes	—
Electricity	40
Gas	10
Water	10
Sanitation	10
Telephone	25
Maintenance	—
Other	—
TOTAL	$255

H-10, Apartment

Description: two bedrooms, two baths, family room (no air conditioning).

Monthly Costs:

Rent	$180
Insurance	10
Taxes	—
Electricity	40
Gas	—
Water	10
Sanitation	10
Telephone	25
Maintenance	—
Other	—
TOTAL	$275

H-11, Apartment

Description: two bedrooms, one-and-a-half baths, air conditioning, laundry room use, pool privileges.

Monthly Costs:

Rent	$200
Insurance	10
Taxes	—
Electricity	40
Gas	10
Water	10
Sanitation	—
Telephone	25
Maintenance	—
Other	—
TOTAL	$295

H-12, Apartment

Description: one bedroom, one bath, air conditioning, nice lot, close to shopping.

Monthly Costs:

Rent	$210
Insurance	15
Taxes	—
Electricity	50
Gas	—
Water	—
Sanitation	—
Telephone	25
Maintenance	—
Other	—
TOTAL	$300

4. Food

The suggested allocation for this category is 16 percent of your NSI.

EXAMPLE: Net Spendable Income = $1,500/month
($1,500 X .16 = $240)
Allocation = $240/month

5. Auto

Before selecting your auto, be sure you have established the percentage and amount you want to spend on a car. If you are not able to get the car you want for that price, you will have to adjust your categories. But remember, the total of all categories cannot exceed 100 percent of your NSI.

A-1, Camaro

Description: V6, power steering, power brakes, 2+2, air conditioning.
Price: $14,000
Down payment: $2,500

Monthly Costs:
Payments	$135
Gas/oil	50
Insurance	75
License	15
Repair/replace	50
TOTAL	$325

A-2, Toyota Celica

Description: five-speed, air conditioning, 30 mpg, two-door, red with sunroof.
Price: $9,200
Down payment: $2,000

Monthly Costs:
Payments	$96
Gas/oil	40
Insurance	30
License	20
Repair/replace	40
TOTAL	$226

A-3, Nissan 300 ZX

Description: five-speed, fully equipped, the ultimate in a sports car.
Price: $18,000
Down payment: $4,000

Monthly Costs:
Payments	$186
Gas/oil	50
Insurance	100
License	20
Repair/replace	50
TOTAL	$406

A-4, Ford Truck, 4WD

Description: Automatic, air conditioning, off-road package, fully equipped.
Price: $14,000
Down payment: $3,000

Monthly Costs:
Payments	$240
Gas/oil	60
Insurance	80
License	20
Repair/replace	50
TOTAL	$450

A-5, Ford Escort

Description: 20,000 miles, warranty, air conditioning, five-speed, excellent condition.
Price: $7,200
Down payment: $1,500

Monthly Costs:

Payments	$80
Gas/oil	40
Insurance	40
License	10
Repair/replace	60
TOTAL	$230

A-6, Honda Accord LX

Description: four-door, fully equipped, No. 1 rated car (Road and Track).
Price: $11,000
Down payment: $3,000

Monthly Costs:

Payments	$120
Gas/oil	40
Insurance	50
License	20
Repair/replace	50
TOTAL	$280

A-7, Honda Civic

Description: 35,000 miles, five-speed, air conditioning, excellent car.
Price: $6,000
Down payment: $1,500

Monthly Costs:

Payments	$85
Gas/oil	40
Insurance	30
License	10
Repair/replace	75
TOTAL	$240

A-8, Chevy Monza

Description: 48,000 miles, two-door, sport, automatic, air conditioning, perfect.
Price: $5,200
Down payment: $1,000

Monthly Costs:

Payments	$65
Gas/oil	50
Insurance	25
License	10
Repair/replace	75
TOTAL	$225

A-9, Porsche

Description: 10,000 miles, candy-apple red, five-speed, turbo.
Price: $28,000
Down payment: $8,000

Monthly Costs:

Payments	$350
Gas/oil	80
Insurance	125
License	20
Repair/replace	100
TOTAL	$675

A-10, Pontiac Grand-AM

Description: 5,000 miles, five-speed, air conditioning, four cylinder, turbo.
Price: $10,800
Down payment: $2,000

Monthly Costs:

Payments	$99
Gas/oil	60
Insurance	75
License	20
Repair/replace	50
TOTAL	$304

A-11, Toyota Corolla

Description: 110,000 miles, two-door, stick shift.
Price: $1,200
Down payment: $300

Monthly Costs:	
Payments	$50
Gas/oil	20
Insurance	25
License	5
Repair/replace	50
TOTAL	$150

A-12, Buick Skylark

Description: 86,000 miles, four-door, automatic, air conditioning.
Price: $1,000
Down payment: $250

Monthly Costs:	
Payments	$40
Gas/oil	25
Insurance	25
License	5
Repair/replace	50
TOTAL	$145

6a. Life Insurance

LI-1, $100,000 Cash Value Insurance
Cash value at 65 = $180,000 $47/mo.

LI-2, $150,000 Cash Value Insurance
Cash value at 65 = $270,000 $75/mo.

LI-3, $250,000 Cash Value Insurance
Cash value at 65 = 667,000 $123/mo.

LI-4, $100,000 Yearly Term Insurance
Cash value at 65 = $.00 $9.60/mo.

LI-5, $250,000 Yearly Term Insurance
Cash value at 65 = $.00 $25/mo.

LI-6, $100,000 5-Year Term Insurance
Cash value at 65 = $.00 $20/mo.

LI-7, $100,000 5-Year Decreasing Term
Cash value at 65 = $.00 $16/mo.

LI-8, $250,000 Single Premium Insurance
Cash value at 65 = $55,000 $6,000 one-time cost.

6b. Medical Insurance

MI-1, Comprehensive health plan that covers hospital costs, doctor, dentist, etc. $100 deductible per person. Pays 80 percent above deductible $175/mo.

MI-2, General health plan that covers hospital costs, doctor, medicines ($5.00 deductible), $150.00 deductible per person. Pays 80 percent above deductible $150/mo.

MI-3, General health plan, same as above (MI-2) except deductible amount per person is $250.00, $125/mo.

MI-4, Major medical insurance plan that pays 80 percent after a deductible of $1,000 per individual $80/mo.

MI-5, Major medical insurance plan that pays 80 percent after a deductible of $2,500 per individual $60/mo.

7. Debts

At this point you should not have any debts accumulated. You do not need a percentage allocated for this category unless you borrow money.

8. Entertainment and Recreation

The suggested allocation for this category is 7 percent of your NSI. You may enter a different amount, but your total allocations may not exceed 100 percent of your NSI.

> **Example:** If your NSI is $1,500/month, your entertainment and recreation allocation would be $105/month.

However, this is one of the categories that can easily get out of control if you don't do some internal budgeting. For instance, when vacation time comes, it's hard if you haven't saved for it. And many people who haven't saved for vacation are tempted to go into debt.

It might be wise to allot a monthly amount toward a vacation, an amount for a regular recreation activity, and limit your other entertainment to what remains.

> **Example:** If you had $105 per month for this category you might set aside $50 for a vacation (to accumulate $600 in a year) and $25 for regular recreation, leaving $30 for all other entertainment.

Below are some possible choices, first for recreational activities and then for vacations for which you might save.

Recreational Activities

R-1, Health Club
Description: Provides the best in conditioning equipment, racquet ball courts, and sauna.
Cost: $40 per month per person.

R-2, Golf-Country Club
Description: An 18-hole, championship course with clubhouse and pool.
Cost: $1,000 membership fee plus $70 per month per family.

R-3, YMCA

Description: Membership privileges include Olympic-size pool, racquet and handball courts, fully-equipped exercise room and sauna.
Cost: $25 per month per person.

R-4, Family-Life Center

Description: Church-run health club with pool, tennis courts, and weight room.
Cost: $25 per month per family.

R-5, Tennis Club

Description: Best clay and composition courts, Olympic size pool, fully equipped workout room. Fee includes professional lessons.
Cost: $50 per month per person.

Vacations

Since virtually all Americans take some form of a vacation, you must budget something. If you don't select one of the specific vacations listed below, allow $40 per month and describe your own vacation.

V-1, Bahamas Trip

Description: Four days, three nights in the beautiful Bahama Islands, including airfare and hotel accommodations and catamaran cruise. (Fee does not include meals. Add $70 per day per person.)
Cost: $360 per person. Budget $30 per month.

V-2, Canadian Ski Trip

Description: Ski in the rugged Canadian Rockies. A seven-day, six-night trip. Cost includes all airfare, hotel, food, and lift tickets.
Cost: $1,704 per person. Budget $142 per month.

V-3, England

Description: Quaint, dream vacation. Seven days, six nights, includes airfare, hotel, food, and sightseeing.
Cost: $720 per person. Budget $60 per month.

V-4, Germany

Description: Off-season special. Five days, three nights in Munich. Includes airfare, hotel, food, rental car with unlimited mileage.
Cost: $456 per person. Budget $38 per month.

V-5, Hawaii

Description: Four sunny days and three sparkling nights at the Maui Hilton. Includes airfare, hotel, rental jeep for open day, and scuba lessons.
Cost: $528 per person. Budget $44 per month.

V-6, Camping

Description: Seven days and six nights in a National Forest. Includes

rental of pop-up camper, all equipment, one-day raft trip, two seven-day fishing licenses, park entrance fee, and travel costs to the park.
Cost: $576 for a family of four. Budget $48 per month.

9. Clothing

The suggested allocation for this category is 5 percent of your NSI. You may enter a different amount, but your total allocations may not exceed 100 percent of your NSI.

10. Savings

The suggested allocation for this category is 5 percent of your NSI. You may enter a different amount, but your total allocations may not exceed 100 percent of your NSI.

11. Medical Expenses

The suggested allocation for this category is 5 percent of your NSI. Even though you may have medical insurance, there will still be other expenses that it does not cover. Some of these expenses could include eye glasses, nonprescription drugs, the deductible and 20 percent of the cost of any medical incident, etc.

12. Miscellaneous

The suggested allocation for this category is 7 percent of your NSI. You may enter a different amount, but your total allocations may not exceed 100 percent of your NSI.

BUDGET BUSTERS

In real life, situations occur that are totally unexpected, situations where you have no choice but to adjust your budget to pay the bills, hopefully out of a surplus. It's the same way here.

Following are four budget buster options assigned according to your income and the number of months of budget keeping you have completed. Select the one which fits your situation and work the expense into your budget.

(If you are taking this course as part of a class, your teacher may assign you a different budget buster.)

It is not necessary to open a new month of record keeping to do this. This adjustment should be done at the bottom of your already filled-out records. In other words, it will be one more expense for your past month. Only if you have to go into debt do you need to fill out a new Form 1, "Monthly Income and Expenses," in the process of applying for a loan.

A. **If your annual income is below $25,500,** and you have completed one or two months of record keeping: You just broke your glasses and had to have them replaced for $118. This unexpected medical bill is not covered by insurance.

B. **If your income is above $25,500,** and you have completed one or two months of record keeping: You had an automobile accident where you were at fault. You received a $35 fine and did $1,500 worth of damage to your car. Fortunately, your insurance will cover the repairs except for the $100 deductible. The total cost of the accident to you is $135.

C. **If your income is below $25,500,** but you have done the "For Additional Study" by completing three months of budgeting: A close relative has just died and you had to go to the funeral—$210 for the trip.

D. **If your income is above $25,500,** but you have done the "For Additional Study" by completing three months of budgeting: You just received notice that you underpaid your income taxes last year and you owe $2,100 additional taxes and fees. The IRS will finance the debt for a minimum payment of $250.00 and monthly payments of $100 at 18 percent (APR) interest over the next twenty-two months. (This will require you to fill out a new Form 1, "Monthly Income and Expenses," to include the repayment of debt.)

LOAN TABLE

This appendix is designed to provide you with the average monthly payment required if you need a loan. It is calculated at 12 percent interest (APR) over a three-year repayment schedule.

The loan amount you need must be recorded on Form 7, "Loan Applications," and the monthly payments must be added to your budget under Category 7, "Debts."

For the purpose of this study, what you borrow must be in $100 increments. If you need to borrow an amount other than those shown in the table, calculate the monthly payment by adding two smaller amounts which equal your need.

For instance, the monthly payments for a $2,500 loan are determined by adding the payment for $2,000 and for $500 ($66 + $17 = $83). For an $800 loan, add the payment for $500 to the payment for $300 ($17 + $10 = 27).

(Since the monthly payments on this chart are rounded off, there may be an advantage in adding other amounts, such as the payments for two $400 loans. You'll get no such breaks in real life, though.)

Loan Amount	Monthly Payment (Approximate)	Total Interest
$ 100	$ 3	$ 19.52
200	7	39.04
300	10	58.56
400	13	78.44
500	17	97.96
1,000	33	195.56
2,000	66	391.48
3,000	100	587.04
4,000	133	782.96
5,000	166	978.52
6,000	199	1,174.44
7,000	232	1,370.00
8,000	266	1,565.56
9,000	299	1,761.48
10,000	332	1,957.04

MONTHLY EXPENSES

Allocations

This appendix serves as a guide for allocating variable monthly expenses, showing two sample expense listings. As you would imagine, expenses do vary month-by-month. So this procedure makes your budget a little more realistic.

Some categories, such as housing and auto, had their expenses shown when you selected them on Appendix B, so they are not shown here. This Appendix is to be used *every* budget cycle (one month) until the study is concluded.

Some categories such as vacations (8e) can have assigned monthly fees or variable fees, depending on your choice in reviewing Appendix B. If you have an assigned fee and another is shown in this appendix, just ignore the one shown.

Example:

Suppose in Appendix B you selected Activity **ACT-1** with a monthly fee of $40. Even though month #1 in this appendix shows an expense of $25 under activities, your budget expense is really $40. If you elect to drop **ACT-1** from your budget, you will have a one-time expense of 10% of your monthly activity fee. In this example it would be $40x12=$480x10%=$48 penalty.

For Month #1

Category	Job A	Job B
1. Contributions	Optional	Optional
2. Tax	Assigned (1)	Assigned
3. Housing		
Mortgage (rent)	Assigned	Assigned
Insurance	Assigned	Assigned
Taxes	Assigned	Assigned
Electricity	78.00 (2)	64.00
Gas	20.00	12.00
Water	15.00	10.00
Sanitation	10.00	10.00
Telephone	60.00	40.00
Maintenance	40.00	0
Other		
4. Food (17%)	220.00	160.00
5. Auto(s)		
Payments	Assigned	Assigned
Gas & Oil	50.00	30.00
Insurance	Assigned	Assigned
License		
Taxes	Assigned	Assigned
Maint./Repair/ Replacement		32.00
6. Insurance		
Life	Assigned	Assigned
Medical	Assigned	Assigned
Other		

Category	Job A	Job B
7. Debts - Student Option		
Credit Cards		
Loans & Notes		
Other		
8. Entertainment & Recreation		
Eating Out	40.00	25.00
Trips	0	15.00
Babysitters	0	0
Activities	25.00	0
Vacation		
Other		
9. Clothing		
10. Savings (5%)	Assigned	Assigned
11. Medical Expenses		
Doctor	20.00	20.00
Dental	25.00	0
Drugs	8.00	18.00
Other		
12. Miscellaneous		
Toiletry, cosmetics	5.00	5.00
Beauty, barber	20.00	10.00
Laundry, cleaning	15.00	0
Allowances, lunches	20.00	20.00
Subscriptions	10.00	5.00
Gifts (incl. Christmas)		
Special Education	0	0
Cash	50.00	30.00
Other		

Note 1: "Assigned" means that monthly costs were preselected according to the expenses shown in Appendix B or a fixed percentage of income.

Note 2: These are monthly expenses. The student must break them down into two pay periods.

NOTE: Some expenses shown may not be applicable, depending on your choice of housing, cars, etc. For instance, apartment **H-7** would have no water expense since it is included in the monthly rent.

For Month #2

Category	Job A	Job B
1. Contributions	Optional	Optional
2. Tax	Assigned (1)	Assigned
3. Housing		
Mortgage (rent)	Assigned	Assigned
Insurance	Assigned	Assigned
Taxes	Assigned	Assigned
Electricity	90.00 (2)	80.00
Gas	10.00	5.00
Water	15.00	10.00
Sanitation	10.00	10.00
Telephone	40.00	40.00
Maintenance	0	25.00
Other		
4. Food (17%)	210.00	155.00
5. Auto(s)		
Payments	Assigned	Assigned
Gas & Oil	50.00	30.00
Insurance	Assigned	Assigned
License		
Taxes	Assigned	Assigned
Maint./Repair/ Replacement	47.00	
6. Insurance		
Life	Assigned	Assigned
Medical	Assigned	Assigned
Other		

Category	Job A	Job B
7. Debts - Student Option		
Credit Cards		
Loans & Notes		
Other		
8. Entertainment & Recreation		
Eating Out	40.00	25.00
Trips	0	15.00
Babysitters	0	0
Activities	25.00	0
Vacation		
Other		
9. Clothing	60.00	50.00
10. Savings (5%)	Assigned	Assigned
11. Medical Expenses		
Doctor		10.00
Dental	18.00	25.00
Drugs	14.00	20.00
Other		
12. Miscellaneous		
Toiletry, cosmetics	10.00	5.00
Beauty, barber	20.00	10.00
Laundry, cleaning	15.00	0
Allowances, lunches	28.00	20.00
Subscriptions	10.00	5.00
Gifts (incl. Christmas)	25.00	
Special Education	0	0
Cash	50.00	30.00
Other		

Note 1: "Assigned" means that monthly costs were preselected according to the expenses shown in Appendix B or a fixed percentage of income.

Note 2: These are monthly expenses. The student must break them down into two pay periods.

NOTE: Some expenses shown may not be applicable, depending on your choice of housing, cars, etc. For instance, apartment **H-7** would have no water expense since it is included in the monthly rent.

For Month #3

Category	Job A	Job B
1. Contributions	Optional	Optional
2. Tax	Assigned (1)	Assigned
3. Housing		
Mortgage (rent)	Assigned	Assigned
Insurance	Assigned	Assigned
Taxes	Assigned	Assigned
Electricity	100.00 (2)	80.00
Gas	10.00	5.00
Water	20.00	10.00
Sanitation	15.00	10.00
Telephone	60.00	30.00
Maintenance		
Other		
4. Food (17%)	250.00	210.00
5. Auto(s)		
Payments	Assigned	Assigned
Gas & Oil	40.00	35.00
Insurance	Assigned	Assigned
License	60.00	40.00
Taxes		
Maint./Repair/ Replacement		35.00
6. Insurance		
Life	Assigned	Assigned
Medical	Assigned	Assigned
Other		

Category	Job A	Job B
7. Debts - Student Option		
Credit Cards		
Loans & Notes		
Other		
8. Entertainment & Recreation		
Eating Out	40.00	30.00
Trips	30.00	15.00
Babysitters		
Activities	25.00	0
Vacation		
Other		
9. Clothing	50.00	
10. Savings (5%)	Assigned	Assigned
11. Medical Expenses		
Doctor		40.00
Dental		
Drugs	10.00	20.00
Other		
12. Miscellaneous		
Toiletry, cosmetics	10.00	5.00
Beauty, barber	20.00	10.00
Laundry, cleaning	15.00	0
Allowances, lunches	20.00	20.00
Subscriptions	10.00	5.00
Gifts (incl. Christmas)	40.00	
Special Education		
Cash	40.00	30.00
Other		

Note 1: "Assigned" means that monthly costs were preselected according to the expenses shown in Appendix B or a fixed percentage of income.

Note 2: These are monthly expenses. The student must break them down into two pay periods.

NOTE: Some expenses shown may not be applicable, depending on your choice of housing, cars, etc. For instance, apartment **H-7** would have no water expense since it is included in the monthly rent.

For Month #4

Category	Job A	Job B
1. Contributions	Optional	Optional
2. Tax	Assigned (1)	Assigned
3. Housing		
Mortgage (rent)	Assigned	Assigned
Insurance	Assigned	Assigned
Taxes	Assigned	Assigned
Electricity	125.00 (2)	80.00
Gas	10.00	5.00
Water	15.00	10.00
Sanitation	10.00	10.00
Telephone	30.00	30.00
Maintenance	60.00	25.00
Other		
4. Food (17%)	180.00	160.00
5. Auto(s)		
Payments	Assigned	Assigned
Gas & Oil	50.00	30.00
Insurance	Assigned	Assigned
License		
Taxes		
Maint./Repair/ Replacement	25.00	100.00
6. Insurance		
Life	Assigned	Assigned
Medical	Assigned	Assigned
Other		

Category	Job A	Job B
7. Debts - Student Option		
Credit Cards		
Loans & Notes		
Other		
8. Entertainment & Recreation		
Eating Out	20.00	20.00
Trips		
Babysitters		
Activities	25.00	10.00
Vacation		
Other		
9. Clothing		40.00
10. Savings (5%)	Assigned	Assigned
11. Medical Expenses		
Doctor		15.00
Dental	20.00	
Drugs		20.00
Other		
12. Miscellaneous		
Toiletry, cosmetics	10.00	5.00
Beauty, barber	20.00	10.00
Laundry, cleaning	15.00	0
Allowances, lunches	25.00	20.00
Subscriptions	10.00	5.00
Gifts (incl. Christmas)		20.00
Special Education		
Cash	50.00	30.00
Other		

Note 1: "Assigned" means that monthly costs were preselected according to the expenses shown in Appendix B or a fixed percentage of income.

Note 2: These are monthly expenses. The student must break them down into two pay periods.

NOTE: Some expenses shown may not be applicable, depending on your choice of housing, cars, etc. For instance, apartment **H-7** would have no water expense since it is included in the monthly rent.

For Month #5

Category	Job A	Job B
1. Contributions	Optional	Optional
2. Tax	Assigned (1)	Assigned
3. Housing		
Mortgage (rent)	Assigned	Assigned
Insurance	Assigned	Assigned
Taxes	Assigned	Assigned
Electricity	75.00 (2)	60.00
Gas	20.00	20.00
Water	10.00	10.00
Sanitation	10.00	10.00
Telephone	40.00	32.00
Maintenance		
Other (pest)	80.00	
4. Food (17%)	230.00	180.00
5. Auto(s)		
Payments	Assigned	Assigned
Gas & Oil	50.00	30.00
Insurance	Assigned	Assigned
License		
Taxes		
Maint./Repair/ Replacement	40.00	20.00
6. Insurance		
Life	Assigned	Assigned
Medical	Assigned	Assigned
Other		

Category	Job A	Job B
7. Debts - Student Option		
Credit Cards		
Loans & Notes		
Other		
8. Entertainment & Recreation		
Eating Out	30.00	30.00
Trips		20.00
Babysitters		
Activities	25.00	10.00
Vacation		
Other		
9. Clothing	60.00	80.00
10. Savings (5%)	Assigned	Assigned
11. Medical Expenses		
Doctor	40.00	
Dental		25.00
Drugs		12.00
Other		
12. Miscellaneous		
Toiletry, cosmetics	10.00	5.00
Beauty, barber	20.00	10.00
Laundry, cleaning	15.00	0
Allowances, lunches	25.00	20.00
Subscriptions	10.00	10.00
Gifts (incl. Christmas)	30.00	20.00
Special Education		
Cash	40.00	30.00
Other		

Note 1: "Assigned" means that monthly costs were preselected according to the expenses shown in Appendix B or a fixed percentage of income.

Note 2: These are monthly expenses. The student must break them down into two pay periods.

NOTE: Some expenses shown may not be applicable, depending on your choice of housing, cars, etc. For instance, apartment **H-7** would have no water expense since it is included in the monthly rent.

For Month #6

Category	Job A	Job B
1. Contributions	Optional	Optional
2. Tax	Assigned (1)	Assigned
3. Housing		
Mortgage (rent)	Assigned	Assigned
Insurance	Assigned	Assigned
Taxes	Assigned	Assigned
Electricity	70.00 (2)	
Gas	30.00	
Water	10.00	
Sanitation	10.00	
Telephone	50.00	
Maintenance		
Other		
4. Food (17%)	200.00	
5. Auto(s)		
Payments	Assigned	Assigned
Gas & Oil	50.00	30.00
Insurance	Assigned	Assigned
License		
Taxes		
Maint./Repair/ Replacement	100.00	40.00
6. Insurance		
Life	Assigned	Assigned
Medical	Assigned	Assigned
Other		

Category	Job A	Job B
7. Debts - Student Option		
Credit Cards		
Loans & Notes		
Other		
8. Entertainment & Recreation		
Eating Out	20.00	20.00
Trips		
Babysitters		
Activities	25.00	10.00
Vacation	300.00	
Other		
9. Clothing	100.00	50.00
10. Savings (5%)	Assigned	Assigned
11. Medical Expenses		
Doctor		20.00
Dental		
Drugs	15.00	
Other		
12. Miscellaneous		
Toiletry, cosmetics	10.00	5.00
Beauty, barber	20.00	10.00
Laundry, cleaning	15.00	0
Allowances, lunches	25.00	20.00
Subscriptions	10.00	5.00
Gifts (incl. Christmas)		
Special Education		
Cash	50.00	30.00
Other		

Note 1: "Assigned" means that monthly costs were preselected according to the expenses shown in Appendix B or a fixed percentage of income.

Note 2: These are monthly expenses. The student must break them down into two pay periods.

NOTE: Some expenses shown may not be applicable, depending on your choice of housing, cars, etc. For instance, apartment **H-7** would have no water expense since it is included in the monthly rent.

Monthly Income and Expenses

Job Name _____ # _____

Annual Income _____

Monthly Income _____

LESS

1. **Charitable Contributions** _____
2. **Tax** _____

NET SPENDABLE INCOME _____

3. **Housing #** _____ **(30%)** _____
   - Mortgage (rent) _____
   - Insurance _____
   - Taxes _____
   - Electricity _____
   - Gas _____
   - Water _____
   - Sanitation _____
   - Telephone _____
   - Maintenance _____
   - Other _____

4. **Food (17%)** _____

5. **Auto(s) #** _____ **(15%)** _____
   - Payments _____
   - Gas & Oil _____
   - Insurance _____
   - License _____
   - Taxes _____
   - Maint./Repair/
     Replacement _____

6. **Insurance (5%)** _____
   - Life# _____ _____
   - Medical# _____ _____

   - Other# _____ _____

7. **Debts (5%)** _____
   - Credit Cards _____
   - Loans & Notes _____
   - Other _____

8. **Enter. & Recreation (7%)** _____
   - Eating Out _____
   - Trips _____
   - Babysitters _____
   - Activities# _____ _____
   - Vacation# _____ _____

   - Other _____

9. **Clothing #** _____ **(5%)** _____

10. **Savings (5%)** _____

11. **Medical Expenses (5%)** _____
    - Doctor _____
    - Dental _____
    - Drugs _____
    - Other _____

12. **Miscellaneous (6%)** _____
    - Toiletry, cosmetics _____
    - Beauty, barber _____
    - Laundry, cleaning _____
    - Allowances,
      lunches _____
    - Subscriptions _____
    - Gifts
      (incl. Christmas) _____
    - Special Education _____
    - Cash _____
    - Other _____

TOTAL EXPENSES _____

Net Spendable Income _____

Difference _____

Division of Pay

PER YEAR $ _____   DIVISION OF PAY

PER MONTH $ _____   PER PAY PERIOD $ _____

MONTHLY PAYMENT CATEGORY	$_____ 1st PAY PERIOD	$_____ 2nd PAY PERIOD
1. Charitable Contributions		
2. Taxes		
NET SPENDABLE INCOME (PER MONTH)	$_____	$_____
3. Housing		
4. Food		
5. Automobile(s)		
6. Insurance		
7. Debts		
8. Enter. & Recreation		
9. Clothing		
10. Savings		
11. Medical		
12. Miscellaneous		
TOTALS (Items 3 through 12)	$_____	$_____

Individual Account Sheets

ACCOUNT NAME		MONTHLY ALLOCATION		1st PAY PERIOD		2nd PAY PERIOD	

DATE	TRANSACTION	DEPOSIT		W/DRAW		BALANCE	

Bank Deposits

BANK DEPOSIT

MONTH: _____ 1st: _____ 2nd: _____

Deposit: _____

Category: 1. $_____

           2. $_____

           3. $_____

           4. $_____

           5. $_____

           6. $_____

           7. $_____

           8. $_____

           9. $_____

          10. $_____

          11. $_____

          12. $_____

Total: _____

BANK DEPOSIT

MONTH: _____ 1st: _____ 2nd: _____

Deposit: _____

Category: 1. $_____

           2. $_____

           3. $_____

           4. $_____

           5. $_____

           6. $_____

           7. $_____

           8. $_____

           9. $_____

          10. $_____

          11. $_____

          12. $_____

Total: _____

BANK DEPOSIT

MONTH: _____ 1st: _____ 2nd: _____

Deposit: _____

Category: 1. $_____

           2. $_____

           3. $_____

           4. $_____

           5. $_____

           6. $_____

           7. $_____

           8. $_____

           9. $_____

          10. $_____

          11. $_____

          12. $_____

Total: _____

BANK DEPOSIT

MONTH: _____ 1st: _____ 2nd: _____

Deposit: _____

Category: 1. $_____

           2. $_____

           3. $_____

           4. $_____

           5. $_____

           6. $_____

           7. $_____

           8. $_____

           9. $_____

          10. $_____

          11. $_____

          12. $_____

Total: _____

Blank Checks

CATEGORY # _____   CHECK # _____

_____ 19_____

PAY TO THE
ORDER OF _____ $ _____

_____ DOLLARS

BANK OF _____

_____

CATEGORY # _____   CHECK # _____

_____ 19_____

PAY TO THE
ORDER OF _____ $ _____

_____ DOLLARS

BANK OF _____

_____

CATEGORY # _____   CHECK # _____

_____ 19_____

PAY TO THE
ORDER OF _____ $ _____

_____ DOLLARS

BANK OF _____

_____

Checking Account Reconciliation

Month: _____

A. Add up all your deposits (from your deposit slips, not your ledger).   . . .   _____

B. Add up all the checks you have written. (Use your actual checks, not your ledger). . . . .   _____

C. Subtract B from A. . . . .   _____

D. Multiply the number of checks you have written by ten cents. . . . .   _____

E. Subtract D from C to find your *Bank Balance*. . . . .   _____

Checking Account Reconciliation

Month: _____

A. Add up all your deposits (from your deposit slips, not your ledger).   . . .   _____

B. Add up all the checks you have written. (Use your actual checks, not your ledger). . . . .   _____

C. Subtract B from A. . . . .   _____

D. Multiply the number of checks you have written by ten cents. . . . .   _____

E. Subtract D from C to find your *Bank Balance*. . . . .   _____

Loan Applications

1. PURPOSE: _____
   _____

   Month: _____ Amount: _____ Payment:_____
   _____
   _____
   _____
   Approval: _____ _____
   _____

2. PURPOSE: _____
   _____

   Month: _____ Amount: _____ Payment:_____
   _____
   _____
   _____
   Approval: _____ _____
   _____

3. PURPOSE: _____
   _____

   Month: _____ Amount: _____ Payment:_____
   _____
   _____
   _____
   Approval: _____ _____
   _____

4. PURPOSE: _____
   _____

   Month: _____ Amount: _____ Payment:_____
   _____
   _____
   _____
   Approval: _____ _____
   _____

Insurance Needs Worksheet

PRESENT INCOME PER YEAR

_____
Line 1

INCOME AVAILABLE
Social Security   _____
Investments   _____

_____   Total = _____
Line 2

ADDITIONAL INCOME REQUIRED TO SUPPORT FAMILY

(Line 1 - Line 2) = _____
Line 3

INSURANCE REQUIRED TO PROVIDE THE NEEDED INCOME

(Line 3 x 10) = _____
Line 4

LUMP SUM REQUIREMENTS (OPTIONAL)
Debt Payments   _____
Funeral Costs   _____
Education Costs   _____

_____   _____

_____   Total = _____
Line 5

TOTAL FUNDS REQUIRED   (Line 4 + 5) _____
Line 6

TOTAL INSURANCE NEEDED   (Line 6) = _____

Car Selection Worksheet

1. What type of car do you need (two-door, four-door, truck, etc.)? _____
_____

2. Establish your maximum price range based on your budget by doing the following:

   A. Set the trade-in value of your "present" car at 50 percent of the cash you were allotted for a car at the beginning of the course. (Sorry, that's just the nature of depreciation.) _____

   B. How much can you afford in monthly payments according to "Payments" on Form 1, "Monthly Income and Expenses," under Category 5? _____

   C. Divide line B by $3.50, then multiply this amount by $100. (Payments at 15 percent over three years are approximately $3.50 per $100.) _____

   D. Add line A and line C to determine your maximum price range.
   _____

3. What equipment do you need (air conditioning, automatic, power steering, etc.)?
_____

4. Using the automotive ads (by dealers) and the classified ads (from private individuals) in the available newspapers, find three cars in your price range that would fill your needs. Where mileage is not given, estimate 12,000 per year unless the ad says "low mileage", in which case then estimate 10,000. (The "rating" is determined in the next step.)

Type	Year	Mileage	Price	Rating

5. Look up those three cars by make and model in a consumer products rating service such as *Consumer Reports* magazine's "Annual Auto Issue" or their "Buying Guide." Rate the cars by placing a "1" by the best, a "2" by the next best, and a "3" by the poorest value.

6. What is *your* first choice? _____

7. If you chose something other than the "first" rated car, explain why. (For instance: price, age, mileage, or personal preference.) _____
_____

What Home Can You Buy?

The monthly payments on a 10.5 percent, thirty-year mortgage average $9.15 per $1,000 of borrowed money. To find a home you can buy, work through the following steps.

1. List your NSI from Form 1, your "Monthly Income and Expenses." _____

2. Calculate 30 percent of this amount to determine how much you can spend on housing. (.30 x your NSI.) _____

3. Of course, not all of that money can be used for mortgage payments. Utilities, insurance, and taxes must come out of it, too. Assume 60 percent of your housing allotment can go for the mortgage. (.60 x Line 2) _____

4. To calculate how much you can borrow for this monthly payment (assuming a 10.5 percent mortgage over thirty years) divide Line 3 by $9.15 and then multiply that amount by 1,000. This is the size of a mortgage that you can afford. _____

5. Add to Line 4 the cash you saved for a home. It was given in Lesson 1 with your job description. _____

6. Subtract $3,000 from Line 5 as an estimated amount for closing costs. This is the price of a home you can afford. _____

7. Look in the real estate section of a local newspaper and see if you can find three homes or condominiums for this amount. List their price and a brief description below.

_____

_____

_____

FORM 11

Creating Your Resumé

Fill in the information below.

NAME: _____

Address: _____

City/State/Zip: _____

Phone: _____

EDUCATION: _____

_____

_____

_____

_____

_____

_____

_____

EXPERIENCE: _____

_____

_____

_____

_____

_____

_____

_____

_____

_____

_____

_____

**ACTIVITIES/
INTERESTS:** _____

_____

_____

_____

_____

_____

_____

REFERENCES: _____

_____

_____

GET A GRIP ON YOUR MONEY   **125**

QUIZ ANSWERS

Lesson 3:   1—F, 2—T, 3—T, 4—B, 5—C.

Lesson 5:   1—F, 2—F, 3—T, 4—C, 5—D.

Lesson 6:   1—T, 2—F, 3—T, 4—C, 5—D.

Lesson 7:   1—F, 2—F, 3—F, 4—B, 5—D, 6—A, 7—C.
Note on Question 3—Most people need about ten
times the income not provided through other
sources.

Lesson 8:   1—F, 2—T, 3—T, 4—F, 5—T, 6—D, 7—B.

Lesson 9:   1—F, 2—T, 3—F, 4—F, 5—B, 6—C, 7—T, 8—A, 9—C.

Lesson 10:   1—F, 2—T, 3—F, 4—F, 5—T, 6—T, 7—C.

Lesson 12:   1—C, 2—I, 3—A, 4—G, 5—F, 6—T, 7—F, 8—F, 9—F,
10—T, 11—F, 12—A, 13—D, 14—B, 15—C.

Lesson 13:   1—F, 2—T, 3—F, 4—F, 5—T, 6—sacrificially, 7—C.